LEARNED HELPLESSNESS:
The Poison Pill Threat to Black America

Colonel Vaughan Witten, Ph.D.

Copyright © 2024 by Colonel Vaughan Witten PhD

All rights reserved. No part of this publication may be reproduced, distributed, or transmitted in any form or by any means, including photocopying, recording, or other electronic or mechanical methods, without the prior written permission of the copyright owner and the publisher, except in the case of brief quotations embodied in critical reviews and certain other noncommercial uses permitted by copyright law. For permission requests, write to the publisher, "Attention: Permissions Coordinator," to the address below.

Studio of Books LLC
5900 Balcones Drive Suite 100
Austin, Texas 78731
www.studioofbooks.org
Hotline: (254) 800-1183

Ordering Information:
Special discounts are available on quantity purchases by corporations, associations, and others. For details, contact the publisher at the address above.

Printed in the United States of America.

ISBN-13:   Hardcover   978-1-964864-25-9

Library of Congress Control Number: 2024913280

LEARNED HELPLESSNESS

The Poison Pill Threat

To

Black America

Colonel Vaughan Witten

United States of America

CONTENTS

LEARNED HELPLESSNESS

Chapter 1 Introduction

2. Franz Fanon-Negro Psychology 8
3. Cognitive Style 11
4. Fear of Success 16
5. Education 22
6. Religion 34
7. Health 44
8. Slavery 50
9. Crime, Malefactors, and the Criminal Industrial Complex 59
10. Culture: American and African 72
11. Low Hanging Fruit 87
Addendum 99
References 125

INTRODUCTION
Chapter One

Learned helplessness is behavior typical of a human or non-human animal that occurs when an animal or human endures repeatedly painful or otherwise aversive stimuli which it is unable to escape or avoid. After such experience the organism often fails to learn or accept "escape" or "avoidance" in new situations where such behavior would likely be effective. In other words the person or organism LEARNED that it is helpless in situations where there is a presence of aversive stimuli and has accepted that it has lost control. Such an organism is said to have acquired learned helplessness, Maier,S.F and Seligman, M.E.P,(1995). Learned helplessness theory is the view that clinical or group depression, related mental illnesses and anti-social behavior may result from such real or perceived absence of control over the outcome of a situation . After multiple aversive stimuli elicited by escape behavior occurs, the punishment is removed and escape is openly possible- such as training and opportunity in a human poverty situation- many will avoid the opportunity to escape, due to the conditioning of previous painful results of previous trying. They just surrender to being helpless.

The thesis of this book is to adapt this theory to my previous research, observations and world view to the proposition that this construct supports my hypothesis that many Black Americans are trapped in poverty, fear, depression, apathy and the ghetto as the result of cultural conditioning that has led them to Escape from Freedom in order to avoid the anxiety, lack of control and uncertainty of Freedom. YES, it sounds counter intuitive to common sense that one would refuse to leave a painful and hopeless situation out of fear of a novel and more beneficial one because of the uncertainty that they may not be able to adapt and survive there as well as they are currently, all the while complaining about it.

They would prefer to be a Big Fish in a small pond rather than a small fish in a Large ocean that may not be as comfortable as their painful "cocoon". Because the unknown and uncertain environment creates anxiety, it may appear to be that the "devil" that I know, though it is bad and gives me at least minimal survival resources, is better than the perceived "devil" that I don't know- though it may be much better once one adapts and adjusts to the reality of the possibility of a richer and much more productive life. They will often shun and fear opportunity to succeed if it does not guarantee the desired results. In America we effectively have a zero sum game of winners and losers. We get no participation trophies. One must work, in most cases for security and success. It is up to the individual will, education, perseverance, and yes some times social status and even luck. But the bottom

Line is that one must play the game if you want to win the game. Spectators have no say- they don't run the ball shoot the ball or hit the ball. To do that one must be on the "field or the court".

Hiroto's,(1975) research revealed that a humans reaction to feeling a lack of control differ both between individuals and between situations, e.g; learned helplessness sometimes remains specific to one situation but at other times generalizes across situations. Such variations were not explained in Seligman's(1972) theory but Hiroto determined such variations depends on an individuals attributional or explanatory style. In other words how does the person perceive or interpret the aversive, painful stimuli or situation as permanent-never changing or temporary and he can do something about it. If one has a pessimistic explanatory style that perceives permanency – then they are likely to suffer from depression and learned helplessness. Hammack,(2011) provides research findings that there is also a neurobiological component involved in learned helplessness. He cites the neurotransmitter 5HT Serotonin. Neurotransmitters are brain chemicals that allows the brain cells to communicate and run the business of the brain and the body. Serotonin in low levels is known to cause depression, suicidal thoughts and obsessive-compulsive disorder, OCD. Just an aside, the transmitter Dopamine that controls minor motor(muscle) activity and regulates the brain pleasure center, is affected by the drugs like cocaine, heroin, opium, nicotine and even alcohol. Increased levels of Dopamine makes a person feel "good", high or euphoric. Too much is strongly associated with the mental disease schizophrenia and too little in involved in Parkinson disease. But enough chemistry for now. Back to the primary topic. If we are to be actually(defacto) free or just (de Jury) legally free- on the books, so to speak, we must change our behavior and world view of victimism, gaming the system, "getting over" and drop the entitlement mentality. We must get rid of all these smart phones, texting, and learn to or be- reading- books, anything. You know that many people believe and with good reason "that if you want to keep a secret from a Black person, write it down". We must take responsibility for our errors, lack of success and stop blaming the white man for everything. He has his own problems and is not overly concerned or thinking about us- of course unless we are trying to rob or kill him. But then he doesn't have to worry too much about that since most black crime occurs against other blacks especially murder, for 95% of blacks murdered are committed by other blacks. About 15% of white murders are committed by blacks. I guess after we get through killing each other, we don't much time left to kill the white man. I suppose he appreciates that. We must stop using drugs and alcohol as a remedy, tape or other devises to close the hole in our soul. There are many factors that have placed us in this dilemma, and will be discussed later in other chapters.

Most behavior is learned, and anything learned can be unlearned-it's a matter of will, incentive, faith and hope. Our (black) intelligence is adequate, though testing has shown an average 15 point low gap compared to whites but some of that can be attributed to culture bias tests. So if we take that off the table as a major factor for our problems, what is the problem. It appears it is our inability to apply our- selves to use analytic thinking in a linear thinking- culture. An Achilles heel? Perhaps. Our criminals are smart, but not smart enough to stay out of jail. One might say that we are "low hanging fruit" in this culture, easy pickings for failure and understanding that this life in America is not designed to guarantee desired results to anyone that cannot or will not make the effort or sacrifice to achieve success. Psychology may be a factor.

Chapter Two

Franz Fanon-Negro Psychology

Franz Fanon, (1925-1961), a Black West Indian psychiatrist and philosopher, born in Fort de France, Martinique in the Caribbean, is well known for his theory that some neuroses are socially generated, based largely on his observations of the violent social control policy and treatment of Martinique natives during the second world war by the Free French Navy who took over the island, after being trapped there by the Nazi's. The Navy established their own government after Hitler defeated France in 1940, and established a puppet government in Southern France and allowed the defeated French to govern themselves as long as they obeyed Nazi rulers in the north. This was the VICHY government in the so called "Free French" in the south. This then affected French colonies around the world such as Martinique, and turned their world upside down.

Fanon was appalled at the master-slave social system employed by the French Navy oppressors. He applied psychoanalysis and psychoanalytic theory to explain the feelings of dependency and inadequacy that Black people experience in a White world. That the divided self perception of the Black subject who has lost his native cultural origin, and embraced the culture of the mother country (France), produce an inferiority complex in the mind of the Black subject, who will then attempt to appropriate and imitate the culture of the colonizer. F.Fanon, Black Skin,White Mask,(1952). Fanon continues, that in this case, colonized Martinique Black people were unable to fit into the norms, (social, cultural, racial) established by white society. That a normal Negro family, will become abnormal on the slightest contact with the white world. That in a

White society, such an extreme psychological response originates from the unconscious any unnatural training in Black people from early childhood, to associate "blackness" with "wrongness". That such unconscious mental training of Black children is effected in comic books, movies, cartoons and books which are cultural media that instill in the mind of the White child that Blacks are villians-and this mental wound becomes inherent in the individual behavioral makeup of the Black personality,(IBID,1952). For Fanon, the White deceiver wore the "White Mask" of superiority for which the "Black Skins" aspired to be like. This dissonance and psychic conflict of attempting to attain the unattainable, generates mental illness,(IBID). This analysis by Fanon fits strongly into my assumptions and hypothesis associated with learning to be helpless in the face of social domination and control, as many Blacks are in America.

CHAPTER THREE

Cognitive Style

Cognitive style or "thinking style" is a term used in Cognitive Psychology to describe the way people think, perceive and remember information. Cognitive style differs from cognitive ability, or intelligence, if you will. The latter being measured by aptitude tests or so called intelligence tests. There is controversy over the exact meaning of the term "cognitive style" and whether it is a single or multiple dimension of human personality.

Without going too deep into the "weeds" of the various theories explaining cognitive style, I will illustrate Witkin's, (1971) theory of Field- Dependence-Field Independence as the basis for my proposal or hypothesis that it is one of the key variables in Black peoples thinking as opposed to White peoples thinking. I must also reveal that this theory was the core basis of my 12 hypotheses on this subject that I proposed regarding my dissertation at North Carolina State University in obtaining my PhD in Psychology after 8 years of study in 1989. By the way I successfully proved 11 of my 12 hypotheses at the 95% level or higher at my defense hearing and missed the 12th one only by one percent. I PASSED.

The Field Dependent-Field Independent model invented by Witkin,(1971) identifies an individuals perceptive behavior while distinguishing object figures from the content field in which they are set. In his embedded figures tests the content field is a distracting or confusing background. These instruments were designed to distinguish Field Dependent from Independent cognitive types with scores of 0-5 indicating field dependency and 6-10, those with higher levels of field independence, that is able to concentrate, function, and perform linear and circular tasks when in a confusing, distracting environment. Further research in this area found that among the multiple variables- race is a significant indicator as a predictor of dependency- with Blacks in general being significantly more dependent or non-autonomous in restructuring skills than Whites, Witten, C. (1989).

Herman A. Witkin's,(1971) Group Embedded Figures Test of finding geometric shapes in a larger design has become a recognized tool for exploring analytical ability, social behavior, body concept prefered defense mechanisms and problem solving styles. Witkin also found that Field Independents tend to prefer to work alone and are internally motivated whearas Field Dependent persons tend to need motivation from others and prefer to work within groups.

Conceptual Systems theory developed by David Hunt et al,(1961) describes the Field Dependent person as experiencing his surroundings in a relatively "global" manner, passively conforming to the influence of the prevailing field or context.

Such an individual tends to see the whole rather than parts of situations. The Field Independent person the other hand experiences the environment "analytically" with objects separate from their background. In this regard, the Field Dependent person only sees the "forest", whereas the Field Independent person sees the "trees" as well as the forest, Witten,(1989). These individual differences in cognative styles are a very congruent fit in my basic thesis that the Black race in America in most social situations as seeing in most cases, only the "forest" so to speak, that is they tend to interpret or "see" or relate to the more superficial, ambiguous and global results of events without knowledge of the relevant, important, facts and chronology of how, and why such event occurred. Their response tends to have a strong emotional component with feelings of pain, condemnation and disappointment when encountering failure or aversive situations without objective analysis or understanding of the actual reality or cause of the event or situation. We "Blacks" tend to dial up denial, excuses, emotion and rationalization in response to our wrong doing or crime by the malefactors that we love.

We raise our young without teaching them manners, self- discipline, respect for authority or hardly any of the customs and conventions of whats necessary for a civilized society to exist. Our young men are essentially cannon fodder for the prison-criminal industrial complex. Then when they end up on drugs, prison or the grave yard-we blame the White man, the Boogeyman the anybody but ourselves. WE are the instrument for our own destructtion, yet we cannot see the "trees" (US) for our own delusional thinking and behavior. Some of the reasons for our circular and upside down thinking that has placed us on this treadmill to self destruction will be addressed in future chapters, but we are in clear and present danger, perceiving only the "forest" of doom and not the trees that make it up.

CHAPTER FOUR

Fear of Success

It seems counter intuitive-but why are so many Blacks, and Whites too for that matter, afraid to succeed? It doesn't make sense on the surface, yet the phenomenon exists. Is it that we think we don't deserve success or some latent unconscious guilt? Hara Marano,(2002), suggests that the fear of success tend to cluster around several issues. One core fear that arises from the reality of change is that success will lead to lonliness. That sometimes people fear that success will mean being attacked by their enemies, or besieged by those wanting money or other things from them. He proposes that women especially fear success because they are afraid that being powerful enough to create the life they want will render them unlovable,(IBID). He continues that when one changes the relationships around them, they will be forced to change. That some friends will cheer them on but others steeped in jealousy will denigrate them for moving.

Kevin Hogan,(2017), proposes 5 reasons why people have a fear of success.
1. IT WILL CHANGE ME.
If I achieve that goal I won't be who I am. I will change somehow-lose my personality.
2. I DON'T DESERVE IT.
I'm not worth it. I don't deserve to be a success.

3. I'TS IMPOSSIBLE
4. I CAN'T DO IT.
I lack the knowledge or ability
5. Believe there are others who are better or smarter than me-they will replace or displace me.

Tim Caine,(2017), a California hypnotherapist says " The fear of success is very real because the future is real-we are all heading there- and what we imagine for our future has an enormous influence on us".

Russell Friedman,(2014), reports that the cliché' of fear of Failure is a misnomer. He says that most people are familiar with failure and as a consequence have little fear of it. He continues that "In a crisis we go back to old beliefs and old behaviors".

Since we know failure so intimately, it's that familiarity that calls us home. The real issue is the fear of success, and since we are not familiar with it, we are drawn away from it and back to what we know best—Failure. Friedman's findings indicates that we have difficulty crossing the familiar failure barrier where we are more comfortable and become anxious and fearful of the success domain because we are not familiar with it and fear it to various degrees. But when we break through and get used to it, we settle down and tend to continue the success. David Allen,MD(2014), has similar experiences with this phenomena. He says these people assume they will fail since they never even attempted to succeed, then how do they know they won't surprise themselves. Since nobody ever gets a guarantee of success when attempting anything, we are all faced with this problem. And yet many of us persevere anyway-why not these folk?,(IBID).

This is a wise observation and conclusion. Why don't some people surrender to failure and quit the pursuit of success? But these people seem to be more comfortable with failure. In the case of the ghetto Black it fits well within the view that they prefer to re- main in the familiar, comfortable, situation of dependence on the welfare system (failure) than explore the unknown, insecure, non-guaranteed venue of possible success and freedom from circular thinking and behavior leading to no where. Allen says these people almost go out of their way to be failures. He continues, that by failing- they are actually succeeding in staying where they are in their cocoon of comfort,(IBID). EBT card, food stamps, free lunch, section 8 housing, no paying taxes, and other freebies available to "victims", are my tangible application to this observation. Tim Caine,(2017), concludes that our culture is focused on the past and we are in effect driving through life looking through the rear view mirror. Finally, Abraham Maslow, (1967) calls this the Jonah Complex where one evades their potential for greatness as did Jonah did by running from his responsability to prophesy the destruction of the city of Nineveh in the Bible, but in vain while being captured by the whale and eventually freed to fulfill his destiny.

CHAPTER FIVE

Education

What is education? What is it's purpose and why is it so important to create and sustain a nation, society or culture? Let's take a look-especially as to how it affects the behavior and world view of Blacks in America.

Education is the process of facilitating learning or the acquisition of knowledge, skills, values beliefs and habits. Educational methods include story- telling, discussion, teaching, training and directed research. Education can take place in a formal or informal setting and any experience that has a formative effect on the way one thinks. Also learners may educate themselves. Education is commonly divided into stages of preschool, primary school, secondary-high school, college-university and apprentiship. The word "Education" is derived from Latin Educatio, (a breeding, a bringing up, a rearing). In preliterate society this was achieved orally and through imitation to train the young in knowledge-skills deemed necessary in their society. In the United States, government supported and free public schools for all, began to be established after the American Revolution, although religious and private schools began soon after the Pilgrims arrived in 1620. In fact Harvard school (University) was founded in 1636 in Massachusetts. Between 1750 and 1870 many Catholic, Jewish, Lutheran and Calvinist parochial schools appeared on the landscape. States passed laws making schools compulsory between 1852 (Massachusetts) and 1917 (Mississippi). In 1862 under President Abraham Lincoln the Merrill Land Grant College Act set up land grant colleges specializing in Agriculture and Engineering with federal funding. By 1870, every state had free elementary schools, (U.S. Department of

Education, (2016). These land grant colleges were typically called "cow colleges" or in many cases "A&T" for Agricultural and Technical, such as N.C.A&T or Texas A&M., Agricultural and Mechanical. In 1946 the National School Lunch Act provided free low cost meals to qualified low income students-on the idea that a "full stomach" supported class attention and learning. This program is still in operation today, (IBID). By 2016 there were about 81 million students enrolled from kindergarten to graduate school, with 85% of adults completing high school and 27% completing a bachelors degree or higher, U.S. Dept. of Education,(IBID). Though the U.S. literacy rate is claimed to be 99%, many including a significant number of Blacks actually cannot effectively read because they do not understand what they see and mimic from the printed page. Juan Cole's,(2017)report on Black education indicates that 14.4% of Black students drop out of high school by age 25, while the number for White students is 7.5%. He says that racism is part of the problem leading to drop outs and that many are actually pushed out by aggressive discipline and suspensions for skipping class, writing on lockers and marijuana in back packs. He reveals that in2012 the U.S. Dept. of Education reported that Blacks made up 18% of the population of schools studed, they made up 35% of those suspended and 37% of those expelled.

In a 2010 report from the Center on Education Policy- it found it would take the state of Louisiana 12.5 years to close the achievement gap between black and white students in 4th grade reading, Florida would take 28 years and Washington state 105 years; while the Knowledge is Power program found that there is a 40% attrition rate for Black boys in sixth to eighth grade.

Tamika Thompson, (2015), has found that 54% of black students graduated from high school compared to 75% for whites and that on average black students in the 12th grade read at the same level as white 8th graders, and that only 14% of black 8th graders score at the proficient level. This then results in millions of young blacks unable to understand or evaluate text, provide relevant details or support inferences about written documents when they read them.

Congresswoman Karen Bass;California, (2013) states we should declare a state of emergency regarding Black student education in Los Angeles. She reports that by the time the Black child reaches 2nd grade they demonstrate a learning gap that only gets worse as they matriculate to higher grades. This then leads to higher drop- out rates and unpreparedness for those who do attend four year colleges where most then drop out. I have witnessed this phenomena personally over the past 3 decades, as a professor -where most flunked out.

Linsay Cook,(2015), suggests that many factors contribute to disparities in education. Lower wealth, lower health, lower parental levels of education, more dealings with the justice system and other circumstances create a perfect storm that leaves Blacks without the same educational opportunities as Whites. He continues that lower expectations by adults contribute to lower expectations from the students- resulting in effect- a self-fulfilling prophesy of failure.

Walter J. Edwards, (2017), of George Mason University describes the Black college graduation rate as dismal, with Howard University 60%, Spelman 74%, Hampton University 66% and Tuskegee University 47% as the four best Black

Colleges graduation rates. His report in the Journal of Black Higher Education also indicates that of 53 HBCU,s studied, Shaw University was #34 at 31% graduation rate, Fayetteville State University at #18 with 40% graduating, Alabama State #49 at 20% graduating and at the bottom University of District of Columbia # 53 at 7% graduating.

Mack H. Hicks,(2014), posits that most Blacks should NOT even go to college- that it is a myth to pursue. The parents and students have unrealistic expectations, the students are unprepared while thinking college equals success-Wrong.

Gene Kelly,(2017), says that students already educationally handicapped, choosing easy majors wind up with low paying dead end jobs and crushing student loan debt. My experience with these students over 3 decades as a university faculty member is that about 25% of the students who DO graduate wind up flipping hamburgers at McDonalds or as a check out cashier at the local Walmart. I concur with Gene Kelly, (2017), that most young blacks and whites for that matter would be better off going to a community college to learn a trade skill like welding, brick masonry, carpentry, truck driving, heavy equipment operator or plumbing. That's where the money is. These people often make $65 to as high as $300 per hour- much more than college graduates and many PhDs, lawyers and doctors. I have also observed that many Black youths don't want a job that gets their hands dirty. They like to be "pretty", wear a suit and tie, carry a brief case, perpetrate an image of something that they are not. I found that most Blacks in my experience have a strong need for recognition, approval and power, we want others to like us and give us praise and awards; but many lack the will, industry or the ethos for sacrifice to earn such recognition. When we don't get it we tend to invent delusional reasons or rationalized excuses that they fail because of discrimination, jealousy, and or racism in the case of whites. We tend to lack introspection into our own soul or psyche in the search for equality, recognition, prosperity and peace in our lives. As a means to ease the pain of low self-respect, lack of respect from others, lack of recognition and loss of dignity in our minds, poverty, inferiority complex and guilt of our circumstances, we lash out at the "system" to fill the hole in our soul.

Finally in this segment Camille Pagalia, (2013) of the Wall Street Journal says that what's pushing us towards universal college graduation is "social snobbery" by the upper middle class. She continues that in some ways, the university world is "non-real". It's a think tank, finishing school, con-gradulatory system that feeds the ego. It does incubate leaders who discover things that don't now exist, but only 5-10% do it.

CHAPTER SIX

Religion

According to Pew Research Center,(2009), African Americans are more markedly religious on a variety of measures than the U.S. population as a whole, including level of affiliation with a religion, attendance at religious services, frequency of prayer and religions importance in life. The U.S. Religious Landscape Survey reports 87% of Blacks say they belong to one religious group or the other with Latinos reporting affiliation of 85% and the general public at 83%,(IBID), 2007. This survey also illustrates Black Americans attending service at least once a week 53% and 88% absolutely believe God exists. These church goers were also more likely to oppose abortion and homosexuality.

Compared with other groups, African Americans express a high degree of comfort with religions role in politics, closely resembling White Evangelical Protestants. The religious composition of Blacks were reported 78% Protestant with 59% attending historically Black churches-40% Baptist, 5% Methodist, 5% Catholic and 15% Evangelical Protestant churches. Although an overwhelming number of Americans say religion is important and they believe God exists, there is a growing number that do not,(IBID).

According to Ebony(2008), 11% of Black Americans are now atheist or agnostics with

15% total Americans in this category. An Atheist does not believe ANY God exists ANYWHERE, and an Agnostic says there is no evidence or proof of the existence of God. 6% of Hispanics are also atheists or agnostics.

Of the 15 million Jews worldwide, 8 million in the U.S., 6 million in Israel and 1 million in 98 other countries, there are a significant number of atheists and agnogtics, Matthew Platts,(2015). This was a surprise to me in the research, perhaps to you also. To go a little further in this respect, it is revealed that a Jew is more of a status than a religion. Anyone born of a Jewish mother, has a Jewish grandmother or is proclaimed by rabbinical court to be a Jew is a JEW regardless of what they believe. The religious belief of status is illustrated in the practice of Jewry. Many Christians have converted to Jew and are then as Jewish as one born a Jew,(IBID). Jews don't believe in Jesus. They do not accept Jesus as the Messiah as Christians do. For one thing they say there has been many false claims to be a messiah before and after Jesus. Yes they believe Jesus was Here as a Man but not as the Son of God. To be the Messiah (anointed) one must accomplish the following:(Rabbi Shuraga Simmons,(2016).

1. Build the third temple-(Ezekiel).
2. Gather all the Jews back to the land of Israel-(Isaiah).
3. Usher in an era of world peace, and end

all hatred, oppression, suffering & disease. (Isaiah).

4. Spread universal knowledge of the God of Israel, which will unite humanity as one. (Zechariah).

If an individual fails to fulfill even one of these conditions, then he cannot be the Messiah, (IBID).

Because no one has ever fulfilled the Bible's description of this future king, Jews still await the coming of the Messiah. All past claimants including Jesus have been rejected. Christians counter that Jesus will fulfill these in the Second coming. Jewish sources say that in the Bible no concept of a Second coming exists, (IBID).

So why is this revelation about Jews important in this context? Well for one thing this small 15 million group of people with a 4000 year history have survived and thrived to a large degree in the midst of 7 billion other people in past era's, even including today, who have been trying to kill them, and often succeeding. In the Middle- East, Iran, and the Palestinians today and in World War II, when Hitler and his Nazi's killed more than 6,000,000 Jews along with other millions of Russians, Gypsies, Poles, Slaaves and many others. But the Jews were systematically murdered to exterminate them. Yet some did survive, and now they have their own COUNTRY and own much of the financial world.

What strength, grit, determination, faith and work ethic they must have to achieve so much since 1948 when they became a sovereign nation and after 1967 when they defeated 7 Arabic nations in the 6 Day War to solidify their borders and become a regional power. It is amazing.

Can we Blacks achieve just a small level of success similar to the Jews? Yes I know we don't have our own religion, nor a country or a 4000 year history of common cause, but where is our determination, work ethic, grit, and sacrifice to be really free and socially – financially independent in America. Our slave fore fathers and mothers had the grit, strength, and determination to survive 300 years of slavery, yet this current Black nation can't survive 150 years of FREEDOM, though our chains and shackels have long been removed. It may be that our minds are still enslaved and havent achieved the evolution yet to attain a world view necessary for enduring success. Are we Sui Generis (unique- one of a kind) that cannot as a race apply ourselves to the laws of nature and man to deal with the vagaries of the world social system. The Jews, Arabs, Chinese, Japanese, Caucasians, Aboriginese, Eskimos and most other races and ethnic groups have; why not us. Where is our strength, our resolve, our grit, our faith, our industry and will to move from darkness and despair to the light of independence and freedom. Can we put aside the past and deal with the present and the future? Can we look ahead and stop making excuses and blaming the White man. No he doesn't love us but he is not Hitler trying to destroy us. He has his own problems-lets deal with ours with out surrendering our dignity, ethos and values. If you want to get out of a hole " you must first stop digging".

Religion is part of the solution but belief must convert to action and achievement. WE claim to be religious, but what does that mean in real terms. Does just going to church every Sunday, dressed up, driving our pretty car, fishing for compliments on how good we look and putting some money in the basket make us religious. Can that get one into Heaven? I think Not. The Lord put us all here basically equal in intelligence, and general ability-after that we are on our own and can't wait for the welfare check and other free "candy" to save us or deliver us to a better place and higher status. Just crying about injustice and discrimination will not do it. NO; industry, discipline, will and faith is required for success.

    WE have to grab the "ball and run with it" so to speak, stop playing "checkers" when every one else is playing "chess". Beat the "Man" at his own game . Out work him, out hustle him, out educate him, out build him, out smart him- he will respect us for that and acquiesce to a place at the "table" for us. Once we are in the game, we CAN Win.

Christianity

Christianity fast facts and introduction

Based on the life and teachings of Jesus Christ about 2,000 years ago, Christianity has over 2 billion followers and can be found in virtually every corner of the globe.

Name Means	followers of Christ (Greek *christos*, Messiah)
Adherents	2.2 billion
Place Founded	Southern Levant (modern-day Israel, Palestine, and Jordan)
Date Founded	c. 30 CE
Founder(s)	Jesus, Peter, Paul
Major Branches	Roman Catholic; Eastern Orthodox; Protestant
Practices	Prayer, Bible study, baptism, Eucharist (Communion church on Sundays, numerous holidays.
Main Holidays	Easter, Christmas, saints' days
Texts	Bible (Hebrew Bible + New Testament)

With over 2 billion adherents (/christianity/adherents) worldwide, Christianity is the largest religion in the world. It has dominated western culture for centuries and remains the majority religion of Europe and the Americas.

Christian beliefs (/christianity/beliefs) center on the life of Jesus of Nazareth (/jesus), a teacher and healer who lived in first century Palestine. The primary source of information about the life of Jesus are the Gospels, which were written sometime between 20 and 100 years after his death and became the first four books of the New Testament. The Gospels describe a three-year teaching and healing ministry during which Jesus attracted 12 close disciples and other followers who believed him to be the Messiah (*Christos*).

Jesus' teachings focused on the themes of the kingdom of God, love of God and love of neighbor. Along with some of his teachings, his growing popularity with the masses was seen as dangerous by Jewish religious leaders and the Roman government, leading to his execution by crucifixion. Christians believe Jesus rose from the dead three days later, and in so doing made it possible for those who believe to be forgiven of sin and attain eternal life. Much of Christian belief and practice centers on the resurrection of Christ.

The sacred text (/christianity/texts) of Christianity is the Christian Bible, which consists of the Old Testament (/old-testament) (the Jewish Bible) and the New Testament (/new-testament). The New Testament contains 27 books: four gospels (narratives of Jesus' life), one account of the apostles' ministry after Jesus' death, letters from church leaders (the earliest of which predate the Gospels), an apocalyptic book.

Nearly all Christians regard the Bible as divinely inspired and authoritative, but views differ (/christianity/scripture) as to the nature and extent of its authority. Some hold it to be completely without error in all matters it addresses, while others stress its accuracy only in religious matters and allow for errors or limitations in other areas due to its human authorship.

Christianity has divided into three major branches (/christianity/branches). Roman Catholicism (/catholicism) represents the continuation of the historical organized church developed over the centuries, and is headed by the Pope. Eastern Orthodoxy and Roman Catholicism separated in 1054, when the Patriarch of Constantinople and the Pope excommunicated each other. Eastern Orthodoxy (/eastern-orthodoxy) (which includes Greek and Russian Orthodox Churches and several others) differs from Catholicism in its refusal of allegiance to the Pope, its emphasis on the use of icons in worship, and the date it celebrates Easter. Other cultural, political, and religious differences exist as well.

Protestantism (/protestantism) arose in the 16th century. Protestants do not acknowledge the authority of the Pope, reject many traditions and beliefs of the Catholic Church, and emphasize the importance of reading the Bible and the doctrine of salvation by faith alone. Protestantism encompasses numerous denominational groups, including Baptists, Methodists, Episcopalians, Presbyterians, Pentecostals and Evangelicals.

Judaism
Judaism fast facts and introduction

One of the oldest religions in the world, Judaism is known for its ethical monotheism. Its core beliefs and traditions are shared with Islam and Christianity.

What Do Jews Believe?

Level: Basic

- Judaism does not have a formal mandatory beliefs
- The most accepted summary of Jewish beliefs is Rambam's 13 principles of faith
- Even these basic principles have been debated
- Judaism focuses on the relationships between the Creator, mankind, and the land of Israel

Name Means	of the Kingdom of Judah
Adherents	14 million
Place Founded	Southern Levant (modern-day Israel, Palestine, and Jordan)
Date Founded	c. 1800 BCE (Abraham); 6th cent. BCE (Pentateuch); or 70 CE (destruction of Second Temple)
Founder(s)	Abraham, Moses
Major Branches	Orthodox, Reform, Conservative
Beliefs	One God: Yahweh (YHVH), who chose the people of Israel and who requires worship, ethical behavior, and rituals. A Messiah will come.

Judaism began (/judaism/date-founded) as early as 2000 BCE as the religion of Abraham and of the small nation of the Hebrews. Through thousands of years of suffering, persecution, dispersion, and the occasional victory, Jewish religion and culture has been profoundly influential.

Today, about 14 million people identify themselves as Jews, and nearly 3.5 billion others follow belief systems directly influenced by Judaism (including Christianity, Islam, and the Bah'ai Faith). Modern Judaism is a complex phenomenon that incorporates both a nation and a religion, and often combines strict adherence to ritual laws with a more liberal attitude towards religious belief.

The central religious belief of Judaism (/judaism/beliefs) is that there is only one God. Monotheism was uncommon at the time Judaism was born, but according to Jewish tradition, God himself revealed it to Abraham, the ancestor of the Jewish people. Judaism teaches that God took special care of the Hebrews (who would later become the Jews).

This is a far more difficult question than you might expect. Judaism has no dogma, no formal set of beliefs that one must hold to be a Jew. In Judaism, actions are far more important than beliefs, although there is certainly a place for belief within Judaism.

13 Principles of Faith

The closest that anyone has ever come to creating a widely-accepted list of Jewish beliefs is Rambam's thirteen principles of faith. These principles, which Rambam thought were the minimum requirements of Jewish belief, are:

1. G-d exists
2. G-d is one and unique
3. G-d is incorporeal
4. G-d is eternal
5. Prayer is to be directed to G-d alone and to no other
6. The words of the prophets are true
7. Moses' prophecies are true, and Moses was the greatest of the prophets
8. The Written Torah (first 5 books of the Bible) and Oral Torah (teachings now contained in the Talmud and other writings) were given to Moses
9. There will be no other Torah
10. G-d knows the thoughts and deeds of men
11. G-d will reward the good and punish the wicked
12. The Messiah will come
13. The dead will be resurrected

Moses (1393-1273 BCE)

Maimonides calls him "the most perfect human being", and the sages of the Talmud said that "the Divine Presence spoke from his throat." Yet the Torah also attests that the man who took the Children of Israel out of Egypt and received the Torah from G-d was "the most humble man on the face of the earth."

Moses was born in Egypt on the 7th of Adar of the year 2368 from creation (1393 BCE), at a time when the Israelites were slaves to the rulers of the land and subject to many harsh decrees. He was the third born of Jocheved and Amram's three children -- his brother Aaron was his senior by three years, and his sister Miriam by six.

When he was three months old, Moses was hidden in a basket set afloat in the Nile to escape Pharaoh's decree that all male Hebrew children be drowned; he was retrieved from the river by Pharaoh's daughter, Batyah, who raised him in the palace. At age 20, Moses fled Egypt after killing an Egyptian he saw beating a Jew and made his way to Midian, where he married Zipporah, the daughter of Jethro, and fathered two sons, Gershom and Eliezer.

When he was 80 years old, Moses was shepherding his father-in-law's sheep when G-d revealed himself to him in a burning bush at Mount Horeb (Sinai) and instructed him to liberate the Children of Israel. Moses took the Israelites out of Egypt, performed numerous miracles for them (the ten plagues in Egypt, the splitting of the sea, extracting water from a rock, bringing down the manna, and numerous others), received the Torah from G-d and taught it to the people, built the Mishkan (Divine dwelling) in the desert, and led the Children of Israel for 40 years as they journeyed through the wilderness; but G-d did not allow him to bring them into the Holy Land. Moses passed away on his 120th birthday on Mount Nebo, within sight of the land he yearned to enter.

Judaism

Judaism is the religion of the Jews. There are an estimated 14 million followers of the Jewish religion around the world. Most of the world's Jews are concentrated in three countries: the United States (six million), Israel (3.7 million), and the Soviet Union (2.5 million). Other nations with significant Jewish populations are France (650 thousand), Great Britain (400 thousand), Canada (300 thousand), Argentina (300 thousand). There are 613 commandments included in the Torah, which also includes the "Ten Commandments." These 613 commandments govern Jewish law covering such areas as philanthropy, sacrifices, prayer, ritual purity, dietary laws, and observances of the Sabbath and other holy days. The Jewish system of law, also referred to as Halacha, includes a civil and criminal justice system which is followed by observant Jews. Halacha regulates Jewish life, such as marriage and divorce, burial, relationships with non-Jews and education.

Muhammad

Muhammad is the founder and chief prophet of Islam and the source for the Quran. "Muhammad" - whose name means "highly praised" - was born in Mecca in 570 AD. His father died shortly before his birth, and he lost his mother at the age of six. Muhammad was then raised primarily by his uncle, for whom he worked as a shepherd. At age 9 (some sources say 12), he joined his uncle on a caravan to Syria. As a young man, Muhammad worked as a camel driver between Syria and Arabia. Soon he established a career managing caravans on behalf of merchants. Through his travel first with his uncle and later in his career, Muhammad came into contact with people of many nationalities and faiths, including Jews, Christians and pagans. (Comparison chart: Islam, Judaism, and Christianity.)

At age 25, Muhammad was employed by Khadija, a wealthy Meccan widow 15 years his senior. The two were married, and by all accounts had a loving and happy marriage. Early records state that "[Allah] comforted him through her, for she made his burden light." Although polygamy was common practice at the time, Muhammad took no other wife until her death 24 years later.

Question: "What is Islam, and what do Muslims believe?"

Answer: Islam is a religious system begun in the seventh century by Muhammad. Muslims follow the teachings of the Qur'an and strive to keep the Five Pillars.

The History of Islam

In the seventh century, Muhammad claimed the angel Gabriel visited him. During these angelic visitations, which continued for about 23 years until Muhammad's death, the angel purportedly revealed to Muhammad the words of Allah (the Arabic word for "God" used by Muslims). These dictated revelations compose the Qur'an, Islam's holy book. Islam means "submission," deriving from a root word that means "peace." The word *Muslim* means "one who submits to Allah."

The Doctrine of Islam

Muslims summarize their doctrine in six articles of faith:
1. Belief in one Allah: Muslims believe Allah is one, eternal, creator, and sovereign.
2. Belief in the angels
3. Belief in the prophets: The prophets include the biblical prophets but end with Muhammad as Allah's final prophet.
4. Belief in the revelations of Allah: Muslims accept certain portions of the Bible, such as the Torah and the Gospels. They believe the Qur'an is the preexistent, perfect word of Allah.
5. Belief in the last day of judgment and the hereafter: Everyone will be resurrected for judgment into either paradise or hell.
6. Belief in predestination: Muslims believe Allah has decreed everything that will happen. Muslims testify to Allah's sovereignty with their frequent phrase, *inshallah*, meaning, "if God wills."

The Five Pillars of Islam

These five tenets compose the framework of obedience for Muslims:
1. The testimony of faith (*shahada*): "*la ilaha illa allah. Muhammad rasul Allah.*" This means, "There is no deity but Allah. Muhammad is the messenger of Allah." A person can convert to Islam by stating this creed. The *shahada* shows that a Muslim believes in Allah alone as deity and believes that Muhammad reveals Allah.
2. Prayer (*salat*): Five ritual prayers must be performed every day.
3. Giving (*zakat*): This almsgiving is a certain percentage given once a year.
4. Fasting (*sawm*): Muslims fast during Ramadan in the ninth month of the Islamic calendar. They must not eat or drink from dawn until sunset.
5. Pilgrimage (*hajj*): If physically and financially possible, a Muslim must make the pilgrimage to Mecca in Saudi Arabia at least once. The *hajj* is performed in the twelfth month of the Islamic calendar.

A Muslim's entrance into paradise hinges on obedience to these Five Pillars. Still, Allah may reject them. Even Muhammad was not sure whether Allah would admit him to paradise (Surah 46:9; Hadith 5.266).

Lutheranism

From Wikipedia, the free encyclopedia

Lutheranism is a major branch of Protestant Christianity which identifies with the theology of Martin Luther (1483–1546), a German friar, ecclesiastical reformer and theologian.

Luther's efforts to reform the theology and practice of the Catholic Church launched the Protestant Reformation in the German-speaking territories of the Holy Roman Empire. Beginning with the Ninety-Five Theses, first published in 1517, Luther's writings were disseminated internationally, spreading the early ideas of the Reformation beyond the influence and control of the Roman Curia and the Holy Roman Emperor.[1] The split between the Lutherans and the Catholics was made public and clear with the 1521 Edict of Worms: the edicts of the Diet condemned Luther and officially banned citizens of the Holy Roman Empire from defending or propagating his ideas, subjecting advocates of Lutheranism to forfeiture of all property, half of the seized property to be forfeit to the imperial government and the remaining half forfeit to the party who brought the accusation.[2] The divide centered primarily on two points: the proper source of authority in the church, often called the *formal principle* of the Reformation, and the doctrine of justification, often called the *material principle*.[a]

Martin Luther initiated the Protestant Reformation in 1517.

Lutheranism advocates a doctrine of justification "by grace alone through faith alone on the basis of Scripture alone", the doctrine that scripture is the final authority on all matters of faith. This is in contrast to the belief of the Catholic Church, defined at the Council of Trent, concerning authority coming from both the Scriptures and Tradition.[3] In addition, Lutheranism accepts the teachings of the first seven ecumenical councils of the undivided Christian Church.[4][5] The Augsburg Confession, a Lutheran statement of belief contained in the Book of Concord, teaches that "the faith as confessed by Luther and his followers is nothing new, but the true catholic faith, and that their churches represent the true catholic or universal church".[6] When the Lutherans presented the Augsburg Confession to Charles V, Holy Roman Emperor, they believe to have "showed that each article of faith and practice was true first of all to Holy Scripture, and then also to the teaching of the church fathers and the councils".[6]

Unlike Calvinism, Lutherans retain many of the liturgical practices and sacramental teachings of the pre-Reformation Church, with a particular emphasis on the Eucharist, or Lord's Supper. Lutheran theology differs from Reformed theology in Christology, the purpose of God's Law, the divine grace, the concept of perseverance of the saints, and predestination.

Today, Lutheranism is one of the largest denominations of Protestantism. With approximately 80 million adherents,[7] it constitutes the third most common Protestant denomination after historically Pentecostal denominations and Anglicanism.[8][b] The Lutheran World Federation, the largest communion of Lutheran churches, represents over 72 million people.[9] Other Lutheran organizations include the International Lutheran Council and the Confessional Evangelical Lutheran Conference, as well as independent churches.

Etymology

The name Lutheran originated as a derogatory term used against Luther by German Scholastic theologian Dr. Johann Maier von Eck during the Leipzig Debate in July 1519.[10] Eck and other Catholics followed the traditional practice of naming a heresy after its leader, thus labeling all who identified with the theology of Martin Luther as Lutherans.[2]

Martin Luther always disliked the term *Lutheran*, preferring the term *Evangelical*, which was derived from *euangelion*, Greek word meaning "good news", i.e. "Gospel".[10] The followers of John Calvin, Huldrych Zwingli, and other theologians linked to the Reformed tradition also began to use that term. To distinguish the two evangelical groups, others began to refer to the two groups as *Evangelical Lutheran* and *Evangelical Reformed*. As time passed by, the word *Evangelical* was dropped. Lutherans themselves began to use the term *Lutheran* in the middle of the 16th century, in order to distinguish themselves from other groups such as the Philippists and Calvinists.

In 1597, theologians in Wittenberg defined the title *Lutheran* as referring to the true church.[2]

What is Calvinism?

by Matt Slick (/matt-slick)

Calvinism, also known as reformed theology, is a movement within orthodox Protestantism (/dictionary-protestant) that was developed by John Calvin (1509-1564), a French theologian. John Calvin was eight years old when Martin Luther posted his 95 theses. Calvin and Luther never met.

Calvin was a lawyer who later became a Pastor in Geneva, Switzerland. He was married in 1539.

Calvin produced many commentaries on various books of the Bible, but he is best known for his seminal work known as *The Institutes of the Christian Religion*, a marvelous work expounding Christian theology (/dictionary-theology), which he published at the age of 26.

The system of Calvinism adheres to a very high view of scripture and seeks to derive its theological formulations based solely on God's word. It focuses on God's sovereignty - stating that God is able and willing by virtue of his omniscience, omnipresence, and omnipotence to do whatever He desires with His creation. It also maintains that within the Bible are the following teachings: That God (/dictionary-god), by His sovereign grace, predestines people into salvation; that Jesus died only for those predestined; that God regenerates the individual to where he is then able to and wants to choose God; and that it is impossible for those who are redeemed to lose their salvation.

Arminianism, on the other hand, maintains that God (/dictionary-god) predestined but not in an absolute sense. Rather, He looked into the future to see who would pick him, and then He chose them. Jesus died for all peoples' sins who have ever lived and ever will live--not just the Christians. Each person is the one who decides if he wants to be saved or not. And finally, it is possible to lose your salvation (some Arminians believe you cannot lose your salvation).

TULIP

Basically, Calvinism is best known by an acronym: T.U.L.I.P.

- **T**otal Depravity (also known as Total Inability and Original Sin)
- **U**nconditional Election
- **L**imited Atonement (also known as Particular Atonement)
- **I**rresistible Grace
- **P**erseverance of the Saints (also known as Once Saved Always Saved)

43F

These five categories do not comprise Calvinism in totality. They simply represent some of its main points.

Total Depravity: Sin has affected all parts of man. The heart, emotions, will, mind, and body are all affected by sin. We are completely sinful. We are not as sinful as we could be, but we are completely affected by sin. The doctrine of Total Depravity is derived from scriptures that reveal human character: Man's heart is evil (Mark 7:21-23

CHAPTER SEVEN

Health

Much of the disease and premature death that affects people of all races can be linked to lifestyle choices. African Americans are no exception, in fact statistics suggest that there are a number of behaviors that are harmful to one's health are common among this group. Although smoking is no more pervasive in the black community than the white community; intravenous drug abuse and OBESITY are more common among African Americans than whites, Kenneth Davis, Jr, MD (2009) College of Medicine, University Cincinnati.

It is hard to know the exact reasons for the negative disparity of so many diseases afflicting Blacks at a higher rate than Whites, but for the purposes of this book it is deemed at least beneficial to reveal the situation. We do know that smoking and other tobacco use contribute to diseases such as coronary heart disease, stroke and lung cancer. We also know that obesity and inactivity contribute to many diseases, (IBID).

HEART DISEASE

In 2013, Black men were killed at a rate of 136 out of 100,000 while White men were killed at a rate of 95 per 100,00. There were 42 deaths from stroke per 100,000 for African Americans compared to 23 per

100,000 for Whites.

CANCER

African American men are at least 50% more likely to develop lung cancer than White men. Also Black men die more often from lung cancer and bronchus than White men, 100 compared to 75 per 100,000 for Whites. Black men are also twice as likely to be diagnosed with prostate cancer as White men. As for breast cancer, the rate for Black women is slightly lower than that for White women,(IBID).

DIABETES

African Americans have a rate of diabetes of 33 per 100,000 compared 23 per 100,000 for Whites.

VITAMIN D DEFECIENCY

African Americans have larger amounts of melanin which filters sunlight,(because of the black skin), and decreases the absorbtion of sun rays necessary for Vitamin D production, Dr. Reginald S. Fowler,(2008). Dr. Fowler continues that Vitamin D deficiency is associated with several cancers and auto- immune diseases such as lupus. There are few sources of Vitamin D other than sun light and milk, and since many Blacks are lactose intolerant- they tend not to drink milk- thus greater deficiency. The only op-tion is vitamin supplements.

SICKLE CELL ANEMIA

Blacks have a 1 in12 chance of suffering

from this genetic disorder where the normal round shaped red blood cell is mal formed into an abnormal sickle shape that clogs up in the arteries and creates havoc in the circulatory blood system. It is incurable and the individual usually has a life expectancy of 50years.

ASTHMA

This is a chronic disease of the lungs and airways that makes breathing difficult. Severe cases can be fatal. It can be caused or promoted by smoke, dust, cock-roaches and genetic disorders. Blacks are 3 times more likely to die from this disease than other Americans,(2005) U.S. EPA.

DIET AND NUTRITION

For some African Americans, a family tradition of soul foods, which traditionally depend on fat, sugar and sodium for their flavor may pose a problem when combined with today's more inactive lifestyle.

| 10 Leading Causes of Death (Both Sexes, All Ages) ||
African American	White
1. Heart Disease	1. Heart Disease
2. Cancer	2. Cancer
3. Cerebrovascular Disease (Stroke)	3. Cerebrovascular Disease (Stroke)
4. Accidents	4. Respiratory Disease (COPD)
5. Diabetes	5. Accidents
6. **Homicide**	6. Pneumonia and Influenza
7. Pneumonia and Influenza	7. Diabetes
8. Respiratory Disease (COPD)	8. **Suicide**
9. **HIV (AIDS)**	9. **Liver Disease**
10. Conditions originating in the perinatal period (period shortly before/after birth)	10. Nephritis, Nephrotic Syndrome and Nephrosis

Source: CDC, National Vital Statistics Report, Vol 48, No. 11, July 24, 2000 (http://www.cdc.gov/nchs/data/nvsr/nvsr48/nvs48_11.pdf)

National Heart, Lung, and Blood Institute

What Is Cholesterol?

To understand high blood cholesterol (ko-LES-ter-ol), it helps to learn about cholesterol. Cholesterol is a waxy, fat-like substance that's found in all cells of the body.

Your body needs some cholesterol to make hormones, vitamin D, and substances that help you digest foods. Your body makes all the cholesterol it needs. However, cholesterol also is found in some of the foods you eat.

Cholesterol travels through your bloodstream in small packages called lipoproteins (lip-o-PRO-teens). These packages are made of fat (lipid) on the inside and proteins on the outside.

Two kinds of lipoproteins carry cholesterol throughout your body: low-density lipoproteins (LDL) and high-density lipoproteins (HDL). Having healthy levels of both types of lipoproteins is important.

LDL cholesterol sometimes is called "bad" cholesterol. A high LDL level leads to a buildup of cholesterol in your arteries. (Arteries are blood vessels that carry blood from your heart to your body.)

HDL cholesterol sometimes is called "good" cholesterol. This is because it carries cholesterol from other parts of your body back to your liver. Your liver removes the cholesterol from your body.

What Is High Blood Cholesterol?

High blood cholesterol is a condition in which you have too much cholesterol in your blood. By itself, the condition usually has no signs or symptoms. Thus, many people don't know that their cholesterol levels are too high.

People who have high blood cholesterol have a greater chance of getting coronary heart disease, also called coronary artery disease. (In this article, the term "heart disease" refers to coronary heart disease.)

The higher the level of LDL cholesterol in your blood, the GREATER your chance is of getting heart disease. The higher the level of HDL cholesterol in your blood, the LOWER your chance is of getting heart disease.

Coronary heart disease is a condition in which plaque (plak) builds up inside the coronary (heart) arteries. Plaque is made up of cholesterol, fat, calcium, and other substances found in the blood. When plaque builds up in the arteries, the condition is called atherosclerosis (ATH-er-o-skler-O-sis).

Atherosclerosis

HIGH CHOLESTEROL

When there is too much cholesterol—a fat-like substance—in your blood, it builds up in the walls of your arteries and increases your risk of developing heart disease. Know your total cholesterol, your LDL (bad) cholesterol, and your HDL (good) cholesterol, and triglycerides. Make an appointment to get tested.

HIGH CHOLESTEROL BY AGE

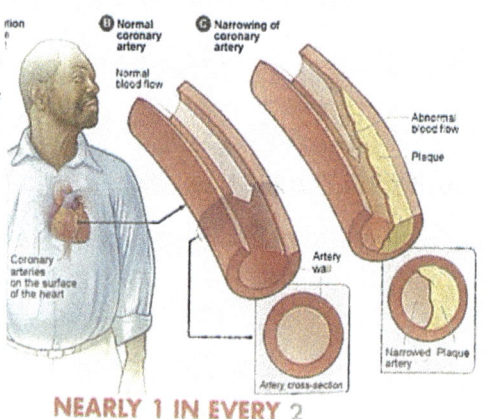

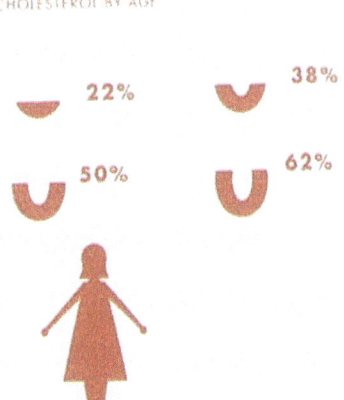

22%
38%
50%
62%

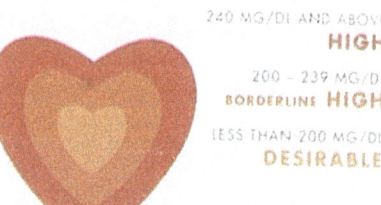

NEARLY 1 IN EVERY 2
AMERICAN WOMEN HAS HIGH OR BORDERLINE HIGH CHOLESTEROL

TOTAL CHOLESTEROL NUMBERS

240 MG/DL AND ABOVE
HIGH

200 – 239 MG/DL
BORDERLINE **HIGH**

LESS THAN 200 MG/DL
DESIRABLE

High LDL can build up and form plaque

LDL is called bad cholesterol because it can build up in the walls of your arteries and form plaque.

This plaque build-up can lead to a condition called hardening of arteries (also known as atherosclerosis, pronounced ath-uh-roh-skluh-ro-sis).

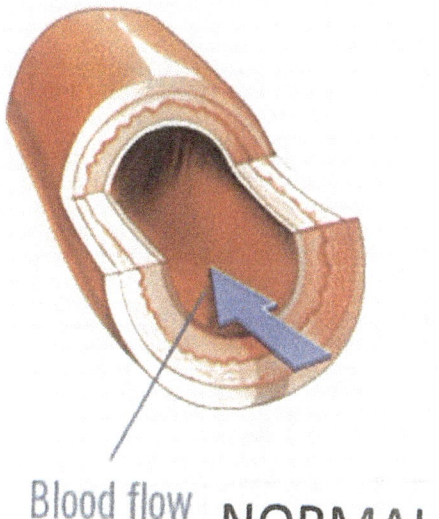

Blood flow — NORMAL

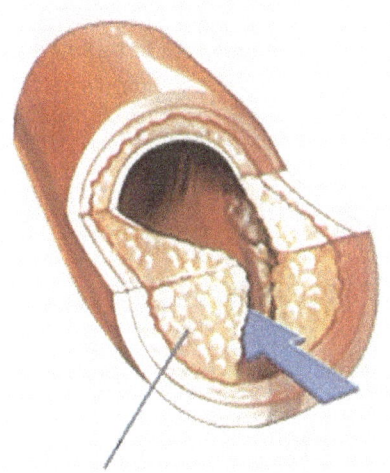

Plaque — ABNORMAL

Understanding Your Cholesterol Level (cont.)

- Cholesterol Levels Slideshow
- Lower Cholesterol Slideshow
- High Cholesterol Quiz

FACEBOOK TWITTER EMAIL PRINT ARTICLE

Cholesterol Charts (what the numbers mean)

Total cholesterol is the sum of all the cholesterol in your blood. Your risk for heart attack and stroke increases with higher cholesterol levels. Other risk factors include smoking, high blood pressure, diabetes, and family history of heart disease or stroke.

IN THIS ARTICLE
- What is cholesterol?
- How are cholesterol levels checked?
- Cholesterol Charts (what the numbers mean)
- What should I do if I have high cholesterol?

Total cholesterol
Less than 200 mg/dL: desirable
200-239 mg/dL: borderline high risk
240 and over: high risk

HDL (high density lipoprotein) is considered the "good" cholesterol because it may help decrease the cholesterol buildup in the walls of arteries that causes narrowing of their openings.

HDL (high density lipoprotein)
Less than 40 mg/dL (men), less than 50 mg/dL (women): increased risk of heart disease
Greater than 60mg/dL: some protection against heart disease

LDL (low density lipoprotein) is considered "bad" cholesterol. The risk of heart disease goes up if you have a high level of LDL cholesterol in your blood because of increased potential for narrowing of blood vessels.

LDL (low density lipoprotein)
Less than 100 mg/dL: optimal
100-129 mg/dL: near optimal/above optimal
130-159 mg/dL: borderline high
160- 189 mg/dL: high
190 mg/dL and above: very high

Triglycerides are another type of fat in the bloodstream. High levels are a risk factor for narrowing arteries in the body.

Triglycerides
Less than n150 mg/dL: normal
150-199 mg/dL: borderline to high
200-499mg/dL: high
Above 500 mg/dL: very high

CHAPTER EIGHT

Slavery

Slavery in America began in the early16th century and continued to be practiced for the next 350 years by the various countries involved in this cruel enterprise. Slaves mostly from Africa, worked in the production of tobacco and cotton mostly in North America; and sugar cane, mining and numerous agricultural crops in Brazil and the many Caribbean Islands. With the invention of the cotton gin in1793 along with the growing demand for the product in Europe, the use of slaves in the North American colonies became the foundation for their economy.

Slavery in the North American colonies

began when the first African slaves were brought to the colony of Jamestown, Virginia in1619, to aid in the production of the lucrative crop of tobacco. Slaves arriving in Jamestown between 1630 and 1640 could expect to be freed after serving their period of endented service, about seven to ten years for Africans and Indians. At this time there was no system of perpetual servitude or slavery for life, but the system was rapidly evolving. Between 1640 and 1660 slavery was becoming a customary reality. In 1640 three servants of Hugh Gwyn, a Dutchman called Victor, a Scotchman named James Gregory, and John Punch, a Negro, having run away from their master were overtaken in Maryland and brought back to stand trial for misbehavior. The verdict of the court would change the system of indentured servitude and set the system in transition to plantation slavery. The court ruled that all three be punished with 30 lashes and that the Dutchman and Scotsman serve out their indenture term plus one year plus an additional 3 years to the colony. But the Negro John Punch was to serve his master for the time of his NATURAL LIFE. This was the first time that color and race became a factor in the status of both black and white indentured servants, Joseph E. Holloway (2015), The Slave Rebellion.

Africans who entered Jamestown between 1620 and 1670 could expect to be freed after serving their indentured time and given 50 to 250 acres of land, hogs, and cows and seeds plus the right to import both white and black indentured servants. For the first time in this brief period a number of African Americans had become freed men and owned indentured white servants. However the Act of 1670 forbad free Negros from owning Christian servants but conceded the right to own servants of their own race. By 1670, it was becoming customary to hold African servants as "slaves for life" and by 1681, what was customary became law,(IBID). And now for a Bomb Shell: Slavery as a perpetual institution is legalized based on a case brought before the Virginia House of Burgess by an African, who had been indentured in Jamestown, Virginia 1621 and was known as Antonio the Negro according to the early records. He later Anglicized his name to Anthony. Anthony Johnson was believed to be the first Black to set foot on Virginia soil. He was the first Black indentured servant, the first free Black, and the first to establish the first Black community, first Black landowner, first Black slave owner, and the first person based on his court case to establish slavery legally in North America. One could argue that he was the founder of slavery in Virginia. In 1635 Johnsons master, Nathaniel Littleton finally released him. As the custom was, he received a 250 acre plantation in 1651 under the "head right system" by which the colonial government encouraged population growth by awarding 50 acres of land for every new servant a settler brought to Virginia. He (Johnson) became the master of both black and white servants.

In 1654 Anthony Johnson went to court and sued his white neighbor for keeping his Black servant John Castor who had ran away to the plantation of Robert Parker. Castor claimed that Johnson had kept him seven years longer than he should so he(Castor) left the Johnson plantation. But Johnson wanted him back. Johnson claimed to the court that he was entitled to Castor for his life. Johnson knew if he lost the case that Castor could win damages from him and he persisted to the court and claimed that Robert Parker had detained Castor "under the pretense that Castor was a free man". The court ruled in favor of Johnson saying that Castor was NOT free and had to be returned to Johnson. Parker had to pay the court costs,(IBID). This case establishes perpetual servitude in North America., and it is ironic that the case was brought by an African who had arrived from Angola in 1621. Slavery was then basically established in 1654 when Anthony Johnson convinced the Virginia court that he was entitled to the lifetime service of John Castor. This was the first judicial approval of life servitude, except as punishment for a crime,(IBID).

By the mid -19th century, America's westward expansion, along with a growing abolition movement in the North, would provoke a great debate over slavery that would tear the nation apart in the bloody American Civil War (1861-1865). Though the Union victory freed the nation's 4,000,000 slaves, the legacy of slavery has continued to influence American history.

Well over 90% of enslaved Africans were imported into the Caribbean and South America. Only about 6% of African captives were sent to British North America. The middle passage was miserable and dangerous. The sexes were separated, kept naked, packed close together, and the men were chained for long periods. Half of all slave infants died in their first year of life mainly from malnutrition. Most infants were weaned within 3 to 4 months, and pregnant mothers worked the field up to one week before childbirth and picked at least ¾ of the produce picked by non-pregnant women. In order to ensure profitability of slaves, and to produce maximum "return on investment" slave owners generally supplied minimum food and shelter needed for survival, and forced their slaves to work from sunrise to sunset.

During the Civil War, roughly 180,000 Black men served in the Union Army, and another 29,000 served in the Navy. 60% of all Black troops were former slaves,(IBID).

The Abolition of The Slave Trade

U.S. Constitution and Acts

Introduction

Before the American Revolution, both the colonies and Great Britain regulated the African slave trade to what became the United States. The British government gave special protection to the Royal African Company, which brought more Africans slaves to the American colonies than any other single entity. The slave trade was an important part of Britain's mercantile policy: it collected taxes on the slaves while colonial governments both taxed them and occasionally sought to limit their arrivals.

After the Stono Rebellion (1739), South Carolina suspended the trade for a few years because its leaders believed that large numbers of freshly imported Africans would undermine the safety of the colony. Then in 1751 South Carolina imposed a special tax on foreign slaves to slow the trade and, nine years later, once again banned it altogether because leaders of the colony still feared the growing number of African-born slaves. The royal authorities disallowed the law. But in 1764 the colony levied new taxes on African-born slaves because, as the legislature noted, their rising number "may prove of the most dangerous consequence."

Shortly before the Revolution, Virginia also tried to ban the trade, not for prudential reasons but to prevent the outflow of capital from the colony. Virginians attempted to use prohibitive taxes to discourage the trade, but the Crown overruled this law, because the slave trade was vital to the British economy and because the Royal African Company had powerful patrons in the government.

The Slave Trade and the Revolution

In his *Summary View of the Rights of British America* (1774), Thomas Jefferson asserted, somewhat disingenuously, that Virginians favored the "abolition of domestic slavery" and that as the first step toward this end, "it is necessary to exclude all further importations from Africa." He complained, however, that "our repeated attempts to effect this by imposing duties which might amount to a prohibition, have been hitherto defeated by his majesty's negative." In his first draft of the Declaration of Independence, Jefferson condemned the Crown in more forceful language, asserting that the king had "waged cruel war against human nature itself, violating its most sacred rights of life and liberty" by perpetuating the African slave trade. Calling it "piratical warfare," Jefferson asserted that "a CHRISTIAN king of Great Britain" was so "Determined to keep open a market where MEN" were bought and sold that he used his "negative" to suppress "every legislative attempt to prohibit or to restrain this execrable commerce."

The Continental Congress removed Jefferson's tirade from the Declaration, in part because it simply did not ring true. The colonists, for the most part, had been willing and eager purchasers of slaves. Nor is there any evidence that either Jefferson or any of the other leaders of Virginia had any interest in actually ending slavery. Virginia's attempt to ban the trade was purely economic, and not based on any moral opposition to slavery. Similarly, the Crown's refusal to allow them to limit or end the trade was economic.

During the Revolution, all of the new states banned or suspended the international slave trade. Most slaves arrived on English ships, and even those on American ships were purchased from agents of the Royal African Company stationed on the west coast of Africa. Thus, all the colonies (which soon became the states) banned the African slave trade as part of their overall policy of refusing to import anything from Britain. The "non-important" movement was an attempt to cut all economic ties with Britain. Since most slaves were brought in by British ships, and virtually all were purchased from the British on the coast of Africa, a ban on the trade was an important part of the colonists' general policy not to trade with Britain.

In some of the northern colonies, abolition of the slave trade had a moral as well as an economic basis. Opposition to slavery was growing, and during or immediately after the Revolution, five states would either end it outright (Massachusetts and New Hampshire) or pass gradual abolition acts (Pennsylvania, Rhode Island, and Connecticut) that would lead to a relatively speedy end to slavery. In those states, a ban on the international slave trade was consistent with growing opposition to slavery itself. In the remaining new states, where slavery was central to the economy, opposition to the trade was economic and political, but not essentially moral. After the Revolution, South Carolina reopened its international trade, but then suspended it in 1785 because of the ongoing depression in the state. Similarly, North Carolina levied a prohibitive tax on newly imported slaves and then in 1794 banned the trade altogether. The trade remained open in Georgia in 1787, but in the wake of the Haitian Revolution, that state also banned it.

The Revolution brought freedom to slaves who joined the armies or escaped in the chaos of war. Thousands left South Carolina and Georgia when the British Army evacuated those states. Some of these people remained free, while others ended up being re-enslaved in the British Caribbean. At the end of the war, leaders in the Deep South fully expected to reopen the trade at some point, to replenish their slave holdings. However, in 1787, when the Constitutional Convention met in Philadelphia, no American state except Georgia had yet reopened the African trade. Nevertheless, with the expectation of reopening the international slave trade, the delegates from the Deep South jealously guarded their right to import more slaves. They succeeded with the provision in Article 1, Section 9 of the Constitution, which prevented Congress from ending the trade before 1808.

The Slave Trade and the Constitution

The final text of the slave trade provision was designed to disguise what the Convention had done. The clause read: "The Migration or Importation of such Persons as any of the States now existing shall think proper to admit shall not be prohibited by the Congress prior to the Year one thousand eight hundred and eight, but a Tax or duty may be imposed on such Importation, not exceeding ten dollars for each Person."

It is important to understand that the clause did not require an end to the trade in 1808. Moreover, it reflected the assumption, held by almost everyone at the Convention, that the Deep South would grow faster than the rest of the nation, and that by 1808 the states that most wanted to continue the trade would have enough political power, and enough allies, to prevent an end to it. Ending the trade would require that a bill pass both houses of Congress and be signed by the president. That process would give the supporters of the trade three opportunities to stop such a bill.

The slave trade provision was a significant factor in the debates over ratification, but its impact was complicated. Opponents of the Constitution, in both the North and the South, roundly condemned the clause. On the other hand, supporters of the Constitution–even those who were ambivalent or hostile to slavery–praised it.

Northern supporters of the Constitution were at a rhetorical disadvantage in this debate, but they nevertheless had to engage the issue. They developed two tactics. The first, best put forth by James Wilson of Pennsylvania, was intellectually dishonest but politically shrewd. He argued that the slave trade clause would in fact allow for the end of slavery itself. In speeches he made the subtle shift from the "trade" to slavery, and since most of his listeners were not as legally sophisticated as Wilson, he was able to fudge the issue. Thus, Wilson told the Pennsylvania ratifying convention that after "the lapse of a few years... Congress will have power to exterminate slavery from within our borders."

Since Wilson attended all the debates over this clause, it is impossible to accept this statement as his understanding of the slave trade clause. More likely, he simply made this argument to win support for the Constitution. Supporters in Massachusetts and New Hampshire made similar arguments. In New Hampshire, a supporter of the Constitution also argued that the slave trade clause gave Congress the power to end slavery. A more sophisticated response to the trade was to note that, without the Constitution, the states could keep the trade open indefinitely because the Congress under the Articles of Confederation had no power to regulate commerce, but under the Constitution it would be possible, in just twenty years, to end the international slave trade. These arguments led northerners to *believe* that the Constitution required an end to the trade after 1808, when in fact it did not.

Upper South supporters of the Constitution, such as James Madison, also made the argument that a ban on the trade was impossible under the Articles, and thus the Constitution, even if imperfect, was still a good bargain. Deep South supporters, like General Charles Cotesworth Pinckney, simply bragged that they had won a great victory–as indeed they had–in protecting the trade for *at least* twenty years. In summing up the entire Constitution, Pinckney, who had been one of the ablest defenders of slavery at the Convention, proudly told the South Carolina House of Representatives: "In short, considering all circumstances, we have made the best terms for the security of this species of property it was in our power to make. We would have made better if we could; but on the whole, I do not think them bad."

Regulating the Trade

While Congress did not have the power to end the international slave trade, it did have the power to regulate it, and starting in 1794, it did just that.

In March, Congress prohibited the use of any U.S. port or shipyard for the purpose of fitting out or building any ship to be used for the introduction of slaves. The law also prohibited ships sailing from U.S. ports from trafficking in foreign countries. Ships sailing from the United States to Africa, even if of foreign registry, were required to "give bond with sufficient sureties, to the treasurer of the United States, that none of the natives of Africa, or any other foreign country or place, shall be taken on board... to be transported, or sold as slaves in any other foreign place, within nine months thereafter." Penalties under the law included fines ranging from $2,000 for outfitting a ship to $200 for an individual working on such a vessel. The act provided that the ships could be confiscated, and half of all fines given to any informants, thus providing an incentive for ship captains and mariners to monitor the activities of anyone they suspected of being involved in the illegal slave trade.

Until 1800 none of the states had reopened the African trade, which had been effectively closed since the Revolution. Before 1800 all introductions into the U.S. were thus illegal, even if the slaves were brought in by foreign ships. After 1800, however, Georgia and South Carolina reopened their international slave trade, and in the next eight years, these two states would introduce about 100,000 new slaves from Africa.

With the trade legally reopened in the Deep South, Congress sought to strengthen the prohibitions on American participation in it. In 1800 Congress amended the 1794 act by dramatically increasing fines for illegal American participation and by giving informants a right to the entire value of any ship condemned under the law. In addition to not allowing American ships to participate in the trade, the new law prohibited any American from having any interest in a ship involved in the trade. Thus, Americans could no longer invest in the transatlantic slave trade, even if carried on legally by non-U.S. ships.

If convicted, an American was subject to a fine that was double the value of his investment in the vessel and also double the value of any slaves in whom he had an interest. The 1800 amendment explicitly prohibited any American citizen or resident alien from voluntarily serving "on board any foreign ship or vessel . . . employed in the slave trade." It no longer mattered if the ship was U.S., or even if it left an American port. American sailors found on slavers were now subject to a $2,000 fine. The law authorized all "commissioned vessels of the United States, to seize and take any vessel employed" in the trade contrary to the law, with the crew receiving half the value of the ship when it was sold. This provided an enormous incentive for American ships to police the trade.

With the trade legal in some states and illegal in others, in 1803 Congress provided new fines for people who brought newly imported slaves into states that banned the international slave trade. The law applied to any "negro, mulatto, or other person of color" introduced as a slave, whether from Africa or the Caribbean. The language was apparently used to prevent people who might bring in Africans by claiming they were not slaves but servants or indentured servants, or claim that they were not actually African but Caribbean.

All three of these laws had been designed to limit American participation in the transatlantic slave trade, but they could not be used to stop the trade itself. Significantly, all of the laws passed before 1807 focused on ships, sailors, and investors. None of the laws had any provision for what should happen to slaves illegally brought into the United States. Indeed, while the 1794 law provided for the sale of a ship and its "tackle, furniture, apparel and other appurtenances" of a slaver, it did not mention what should happen to the slaves or any cargo on the ship. Presumably, they too would be sold for the benefit of the United States, the informant, or any other claimant under the three laws.

In his annual message to Congress in December 1806, Thomas Jefferson, who had long opposed the trade (but not slavery itself), reminded the nation that on January 1, 1808, the constitutional suspension of congressional power on this issue would finally expire. He took a moment in his address to "congratulate" his "fellow-citizens, on the approach of the period at which you may interpose your authority constitutionally to withdraw the citizens of the United States from all further participation in those violations of human rights which have been so long continued on the unoffending inhabitants of Africa, and which the morality, the reputation, and the best interests of our country have long been eager to proscribe." He noted that any law passed by Congress could not take effect until January 1, 1808, but he urged Congress to act quickly "to prevent by timely notice expeditions which can not be completed before that day." Congress readily complied with legislation to absolutely ban all importations of slaves after January 1, 1808.

What Is an Arrest?

Whether a person is "under arrest" depends on the circumstances of the police encounter.

An arrest occurs when police officers take a suspect into custody. An arrest is complete as soon as the suspect is no longer free to walk away from the arresting police officer, a moment that often comes well before the suspect actually arrives at a jail.

What Constitutes an Arrest?

An arrest requires taking someone into custody, against that person's will, in order to prosecute or interrogate. It involves a physical application of force, or submission to an officer's show of force. In sum, the arrestee must not be free to leave. Whether the act by the police is termed an arrest under state law is not relevant.

When deciding whether someone has been arrested, courts apply the "reasonable man" standard. This means asking whether a reasonable person, in the shoes of the defendant, would have concluded that he or she was not free to leave.

No arrest happens when an officer approaches someone in a public place and asks if the person is willing to answer questions, as long as the officer does not restrain the person.

The U.S. Constitution's Fourth Amendment authorizes an arrest only if the police have probable cause (http://www.nolo.com/legal-encyclopedia/what-level-certainty-does-probable-cause-require.html) to believe that a crime was committed and that the suspect did it. This probable cause requirement restrains the power of the police to deprive people of liberty. It prevents the type of random roundup of "undesirables" that sometimes occurs in other countries.

Legislatures and courts have picked up where the Fourth Amendment leaves off, developing rules about how, when, and why people can be arrested. (For more information, particularly about determining whether you're under arrest, see Arrest: "Seizing" People (http://www.nolo.c A person may be taken in custody completely or even partially. The concept of being in custody is, therefore, different from that of a formal arrest. Thus it would be seen that in every arrest there is custody but the converse is not true and as such, arrest and custody are not synonymous

What are the Difference between Arrest and Custody?

Arrest is a mode of formally taking a person in police custody. Whereas 'custody' merely denotes surveillance or restriction on the movement of the person concerned.

CHAPTER TEN

Culture: Africa and African American

Culture can be defined in many ways. The Cambridge English Dictionary states that "culture is the way of life, especially the general customs and beliefs, of a particular group of people at a particular time". As a defining aspect of what it means to be human, culture is a central concept in the science of Anthropology, encompassing the range of phenomena that are transmitted through social learning in human societies,Wikipedia,(2017). The concept of material culture covers the physical expressions of culture such as technology, art and architecture, whereas the immaterial aspects of culture is expressed in the principles of social organization, mythology, philosophy, literature(written and oral) and science-the intangible cultural heritage of a society,(IBID).

The topic of Culture and Personality is controversial. Bruner,(1974) assessed the field as a "magnificent failure". Triandis and Suh,(2002), Schweder(1991) all argued that individual differences in conduct are narrowly context dependent and do not generalize across context situations. Thus global traits do Not exist. Bruner,(1974) further argued that early child care practices per se do not have predictable consequences for adult character. More positive evaluations have occurred recently such as Lee,(1999) and McCrae,(2000) who present a view diametrically opposite to Schweder, (1991), (IBID). According to McCrae et al, (2000), global traits DO exist. They claim that studies of heritability and invariance across cultures and species all point to the notion that personality traits are more expressions of human Biology than the product of life experiences.

Triandis and Suh,(2002), take a more in-termediate position than the poles of Schweder and McCrae and look for universal generalizations, while at the same time admitting culture specific information. For purposes of this (my) conceptualization, I lean to or agree with Maccoby,(2000), and Rohner,(1999), in their view and posit that personality is shaped by both genetic and environmental influences. Triandis believes that culture is the most important factor in environmental influences-which is transmitted through language and modeling of behavior in the same historical period, influences each other. Rohner, (1999) contends when parents accept their children with much hugging and comforting, the children become more sociable, emotionally stable, have high self- esteem, feel self- adequate and have a positive world view. When parents are rejecting-hitting, using sarcastic language, humiliating and neglecting; their children become adults who are hostile unresponsive, unstable, immaturely dependent and have impaired self- esteem and a negative world view.

With this illustrated background it is now incumbent upon this treatise to move to the concept of the real or probable influence of African and African American culture on the personality of the current Blacks in the United States. Black American culture refers to the cultural contributions to the American culture as well as to a distinct Black subculture and is mostly rooted in West and Central Africa. Although slavery greatly restricted the ability of Black Americans to practice their original traditions, many values, and beliefs survived and over time have modified or blended with European cultures and others such as Native Americans. Black American identities were established during the slavery period producing a dynamic culture that has had a profound impact on American culture, Gomez, M. (1998).

Many West African societies traditionally believed that spirits dwelled in their surrounding nature. From this disposition they treated their environment with mindful care. They also generally believed that a spiritual life source existed after death. Honor and prayer were displayed to the spirit or "ancient ones" of the past, Clayborn Carson et al,((2012).

In the beginning of the 17th century, Christianity began to spread across North and West Africa, and this shift in religion began displacing traditional African spiritual practices. The enslaved Africans brought this complex religious dynamic within their culture to America. This fusion of traditional African beliefs with Christianity provided a common place for those practicing religion in Africa and America, (IBID).

After emancipation, unique African American traditions continued in music, art, cuisine, religion and other fields. Anthropologist Melville Herskovits demonstrated that there had been a continuum of African traditions, but 20th century Gunnar Myrdal believed that African Americans had lost most of their cultural ties with Africa. For many years African American culture DID develop separately from Euro-American culture, both because of slavery and the persistence of discrimination in America as well as African American slave decendants desire to maintain their own traditions. Today African American culture has become a significant part of American culture, and yet, at the same time, remains a distinct cultural body, African American Voices: Slave Culture-University of Houston,(2000).

From the earliest days of American slavery in the 17th century, slave owners sought to exercise control over their slaves to strip them of their African culture to prevent resistance or rebellion that took place in the U.S., Brazil, Haiti and the Dutch Guyanas.Yet the imprint of Africa is present in a myriad of ways in politics, economics, language, cuisine, hairstyle, music, fashion, dance and world view.

African basic oral traditions became the primary means of preserving story- telling, mores and other cultural information, in that slaves were forbidden education, reading and writing; to suppress planning and execution of revolts and overthrow of the slave master. The legacy of the African American oral traditions manifests in various forms. African American preachers tend to perform rather simply speak. The level of emotion of the subject is carried through the speakers tone, volume and cadence which tend to mirror the rising action, climax and descending action of the sermon. Often song, dance, verse and structured pauses are placed throughout the sermon.

It manifests in worship in what is commonly called the "amen corner"". In direct contrast to other American and Western cultures, it is an acceptable and common reaction to interrupt and affirm the speaker. Other aspects of African American oral traditions include the dozens, signifying, trash talk, rhyming, semantic inversion, and word play; many of which have made their way into mainstream American popular culture. Rap music from the 1980s and beyond has been seen as an extention of oral culture.

Many Black Americans Sing "Lift every voice and Sing" in addition to the American National Anthem,"Star Spangled Banner", or in lieu of it. This song adopted as the

"Negro National Anthem" in 1919 by the NAACP, was written by James Weldon Johnson and John Rosamon Johnson in 1900 for the celebration of the birthday of Abraham Lincoln, Julian Bond et al (2000).

The Black Power movement of the 1960s and 1970s, followed in the wake of the non-violent Civil Rights movement. The movement promoted racial pride and ethnic cohesion in contrast to the focus on integration of the Civil Rights movement and adopted a more militant picture in the face of racism,Black Power,(2007)

For most Blacks the observance of life events follows mainstream American culture. While African Americans and Whites often lived to themselves through much of

American history, both groups generally had the same perspective on American culture. Today some Black couples choose to "jump the broom" as part of their wedding ceremony, but the practice-traced back to Ghana has fell out of favor for the most part since the end of slavery,Grimes, Ronald, (2002). About death, for most Blacks the entire end of life process is generally treated as a celebration of the persons life, deeds, and accomplishments, the "good things"rather than a mourning or a loss. This is most notably demonstrated in the New Orleans jazz funeral tradition where upbeat music, dancing, and food encourage people to be happy and celebrate the "homegoing" of a loved one Anyiam, T,

(2007), Who Should Jump the Broom.

Under slavery, Blacks were not allowed to eat better cuts of meat, and after emancipation -too poor to afford them. Instead they ate mostly Soul food cuisine: pig intestine- chittlins, pig feet, neck bones, rabbit, fried chicken, possum, rice, fish, ham hocks, corn bread, macaroni and cheese and squirrel. This food was traditionally high in fat, sodium and starch which were suited for the demanding life of laborers. But now these foods contribute to obesity, heart disease, and diabetes as this population has become more urban and sedentary,Hicks,D.(2014).

African Americans as slaves, were often given European names and most surnames are of Anglo origins. Today Blacks names have origins in many languages; French, Latin, Arabic and African. Muslim and African names are now more popular such as Jamal, Malik-Ashanty, Tanisha, Alisha, Katrina, Deshone and Maliaka. Many names are now invented with prefixes of La/Le, Da/De, Ra/Re, Ja/Je, and suffixes of Ique, Iqua, Isha, and Auan/awn; but many still Biblical, historical or European names such as David, Robert, Mary, Jane, John and so on, Wattenburg,L. (2013), Moskovitz,C. (2010).

Many affluent Black communities exist Today in the U.S. including Woodmore,MD., Hillcrest,N.Y., Redan,Ga. Due to segregated conditions and widespread poverty, some

Black neighborhoods in the U.S. have been called "ghettos". These ghettos did not always contain dilapidated houses and decaying projects, nor all of it's residents poverty stricken. This was and Is Home for many and a place to represent "Blackness" and a feeling of emotionally belonging, Payne,J. (2007).

Many Black neighborhoods are located in inner cities, mostly residential and close to the central business district. Ghetto project housing is also similarly located. The upper class Whites and Blacks tend to live in surburbs 5 to 15 miles away. Shotgun houses are also important in many parts of the South. These houses consist of 3 to 5 rooms in a row with no hallway.

black culture pictures

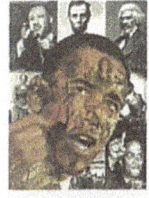

Explore more searches like **black cultu**re pictures

Ghetto Stock Photos and Images

Sort by: **Relevance** Filter by: Image Type Orientation More

Related Searches: casette tape ghetto street

 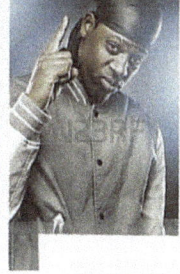 

86C

86D

African Culture Stock Photos and Images

86E

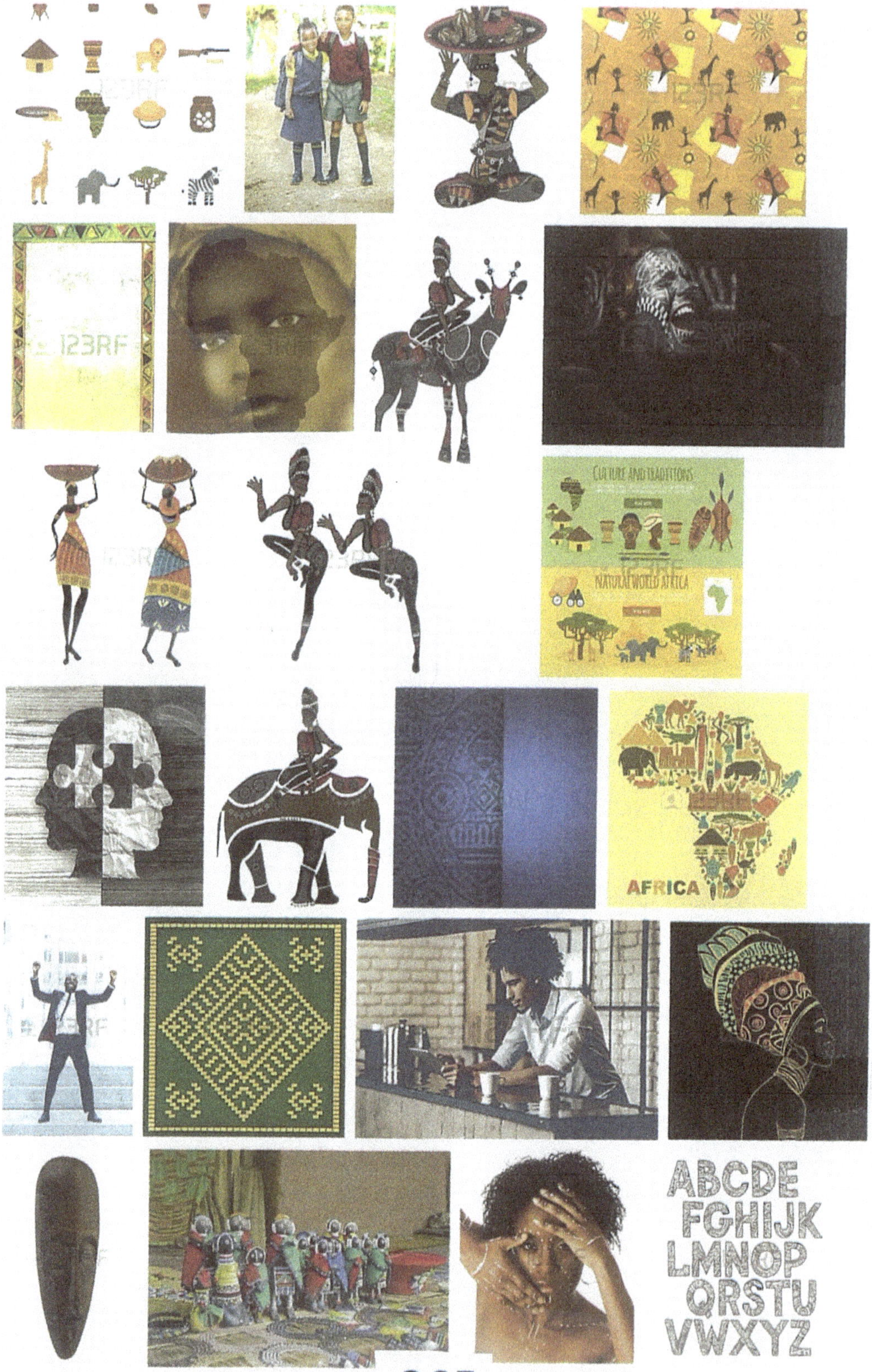
123RF
CULTURE AND TRADITIONS
NATURAL WORLD AFRICA
AFRICA
ABCDE
FGHIJK
LMNOP
QRSTU
VWXYZ

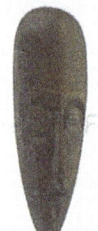

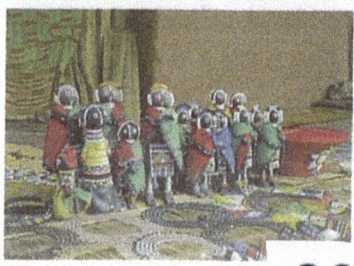

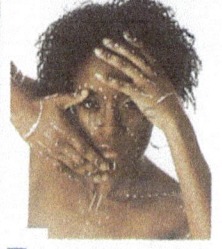

86F

All of these factors and variables are deemed to have an influence on the individuals self-worth, politics, emotional state, education, health, mood and world view: affecting his or her behavior-personality.

CHAPTER ELEVEN

Low Hanging Fruit

The concept or euphemism of the term "Low Hanging Fruit" is based on the notion of being "easy" to take or to influence or predict. The lower the apples are to the ground, the easier they are to pick, so to speak. The metaphor of doing the simplest or easiest work first, for the quick fix that produces ripe delectable results, or that the target to influence is easy to sell, fits many Black Americans spot on.

    What do I mean by the statement that Blacks are low hanging fruit in America that benefits others but not the Blacks themselves? That we are easy pickings for our capitalist system to manage and dominate. Yes, we complain, cry discrimination, rob, kill each other-and occasionally a white person, vote in small numbers, cost the government lots of welfare money and produce lots of criminals for the prison industry BUT it is effectively a small price for the power structure to pay-to Remain in Power. We now look at some categories in which it is Illustrated that this is so.

1. POLITICS/VOTING: We can be counted on to vote around 90% or more for Democrats in most any election, 99% if the candidate is Black. We vote with our heart-Not our head. Everything is emotional. We are attracted to the form and appearance of things, Not it's substance. We are easily conned into doing things against our own self interest without inquiry or scrutiny because the speaker or politician is "cool" or polished, or Black, with no concern for their qualifications or the long term results of the proposals and the reality of the promises being fulfilled. If it is quick, easy and Free, we jump at it, often to our peril. And when they lie

to us we continue to vote for them next time. They don't have to spend much money on us because they already have us in their pocket. So the politicians concentrate on the Hispanics and Whites who are higher up in the tree and harder to pick.

2. EDUCATION: We are easy here also. Our children receive an 8th grade education when receiving a high school diploma. But we are happy and proud, and celebrate. Yes, we should be proud but not happy because we have been duped that our child has a REAL high school education. That piece of paper is practically worthless, most students can't get into a top college and if they do about 75% flunk out or drop out. Most cannot effectively read

write, cipher or infer knowledge or information. They can barely do the work in HBCUs, and barely graduate in most cases with a "C" average, that's worth a good high school education. As long as we continue to allow the school systems to under educate our children right under our nose, we will continue to be "EASY" to dominate in every field of our society, while we are dancing, gambling and squandering our EBT from the SNAP program. So as long as we are content with the way it is without demanding change, the system will never take us seriously.

3. AUTOMOBILES: Cars/Trucks- We like pretty flashy, shiny things, often even when they don't work, are expensive and perishable. You see in many cases we have such low self-esteem, that we have to identify with something else that is valuable, recognized, worthy, or loved which will make us valuable and worthy. To a large degree many of us have been robbed of our intrinsic value, self-esteem and pride; so we get it through artificial and materialistic means, like big pretty cars, jewelry, big houses and for our men – a White woman. So what do we do if and when we hit the numbers, win the lottery, win an accident case or other

wise come into a large sum of money, we run right out and buy a Cadillac, Mercedes, Lincoln or a $70,000 Pickup truck. NOW we are SOMEBODY, and can show it off. Now we can be "seen", recognized, and given some attention which is what we lacked in the first place. Of course the car dealerships love us ☺ ; as we continue on our "bridge to no where" ☹ .

4. WELFARE AND POVERTY: We are EASY PIKENS to continue to participate in the Welfare Industrial complex. Without us millions of welfare workers and politicians would be out of a job. You see, in this context we are important and valuable, for we

keep them employed. They know that we will always be there for them, as cannon fodder for "their check". And for that We get a check, EBT card, subsidized housing and other elements of the SNAP program. Yes, of course we get a benefit of daily subsistence survival, but that is as far as most will go as long as we are content to stay at this level. But the soothing effect of a guaranteed check every month is too powerful a "koolaid", to risk giving up and work our way out of this quasi slavery. To escape this situation is fearful, for one would have to trade a guaranteed survival of a Big Fish in a small pond with the risk of being a small fish in a BIG OCEAN.

5. Disease, Unhealthy Diet and Death.

   We are Easy pickings for cancer, heart disease, diabetes kidney/dialysis, high cholesterol, drug addiction and AIDS. We love our fat back, pork chops, pig feet, hog maws, alcohol, sugary drinks and other killer forms of fast food and drinks. Oh I forgot chitterlins ,☺. Yes, I know much of the preference for these fatty, sodium filled foods have been modeled and passed down to us from slavery traditions, but we now know the danger of these foods that causes most of the diseases we incur, yet we still eat them. The Black male especially-with a life expectancy 5 to 7 years less than a White man and even less for the White woman or Black woman; is most at risk.

Though unhealthy foods are a major component in our early death, murder-homicide is the primary killer of the young Black male 95% by other Black males, with an occasional killing by police-some perpetrated as suicide by cop. One study I recall-absent of reference- revealed that once a Black man makes it to 65, he has a better chance of living to be 95 than the average White man.

6. GAMBLING: We just love to gamble, and are suckers in our effort to get something easy or free. It usually backfires and we lose more than we win-but we keep doing it. The gambling casinos, lotteries and the "numbers" are made to order for us. Many can't resist gambling the rent money or car

payment on some get rich scheme or fancy advertisement that ends up taking our money. And of course we love to buy the scratch off at the gas station. There are so many in line that it is difficult to just buy gas. We are easy pigeons for the deceptive and crippling lies we are told about our chances to win, AND EVEN when we are told the odds are 10,000,000 to 1, we still plunck down our $2. And don't even go to a "free" cookout. The people will be lined up coming out of the "woodwork" to get the free food, and then add insult to injury by taking one or two "plates" home with them☺.

I could go on, but I think this enough. The factors of poverty, discrimination, crime, religion, slavery, health, cognitive style, culture, fear of failure, education and psychology have been addressed in this treatise and examined for relevant strength and influence on our behavior. I admit I have not teased out or discovered the "smoking gun" that has placed us here, BUT we are HERE and it is REAL. We are on a slippery slope to DOOM, and ignore it at our PERIL. The ball is in the readers court and requires some introspection if interested . I am only the MESSENGER.

      Colonel Vaughan Witten, PhD

Low-Hanging Fruit

+ SUBSCRIBE

You May Also Like: Learn to trade stocks with virtual money before you risk your own...

What is a 'Low-Hanging Fruit'

A low-hanging fruit is a commonly used metaphor for doing the simplest or easiest work first or for a quick fix that produces ripe, delectable results. In sales, it means a target that is easy to achieve, a product or service that is easy to sell, or a prospective client who seems very likely to buy the product, especially compared to other, more reluctant prospects. The phrase also refers to a problem that is easy to solve.

BREAKING DOWN 'Low-Hanging Fruit'

To illustrate the concept of low-hanging fruit, imagine a sales rep has been talking to several prospects and one seems more likely to buy his product than the others. If the sales rep channels his efforts toward the easiest sale, he is focusing on the low-hanging fruit. This is also referred to as cherry picking clients or opportunities.

Similarly, if a company implements a strategy to boost sales quickly, rather than an arduous process that takes a long time to produce results, this is also grabbing the low-hanging fruit.

Pros of Cons of Focusing on Low-Hanging Fruit

Businesses or sales professionals who opt to focus on low-hanging fruit are likely to meet their targets faster, close sales more easily or accomplish their to-do lists sooner. From this perspective, focusing on low-hanging fruit can be an effective sales and business strategy. However, in most cases, there are usually only so many low-hanging fruits, and once those have been "picked," the company has to put in more effort to achieve results. Essentially, if a company or an individual decides to exclusively focus on low-hanging fruit, it pushes all of the more difficult tasks onto the metaphorical back burner, and putting those tasks on hold can make them harder to achieve in the long run.

History of the Phrase Low-Hanging Fruit

Phrases such as "fruit low hung" and "fruit hanging low" have been part of the English language since the 17th century, but the exact phrase "low-hanging fruit" likely first appeared in print in a 1968 article in the Guardian newspaper, and the phrase referenced something easily attainable.

ADDENDUM

>Glossary-Black Slang.

>Slavery isn't a thing of the past.

>Slavery Today.

>U.S. ranks first in Prisoners.

>Satisfaction with national conditions.

>U.S. Adult math skills.

>U.S. Rank in literacy.

>FBI Statistics: Black hate crime.

>Black males going to prison in lifetime.

>African American Health disparities.

>About the author.

>Viet Nam maps and pictures-Witten.

>United States map-Witten state visits.

>World map-Witten service bases and country visits-1952-1979.

Glossary – Black Slang

AKA- Also known as

Apple- Indian, Red on outside and White on inside

Africant- Unemployed lazy Black

Benjamin- 100 dollar bills

Bear- Black, educated and rich

Biscuit lip- Large lips

Uber- Extreme, to an excessive degree

Bail- to leave in a hurry

Diesel- Muscular

DWB- Driving while black

EBT- Electronic Benefit Transfer card, aka Food stamp card

Ghost rider- Blacks having sex with whites

Going postal- Going crazy with anger- wild

Hambone- Overweight man

Horse- Heroin

Hillbilly heroin- Narcotic drug Oxycodone

Niglet- A young N-word person

Oreo- Black on out side and white on inside

99A

Pineapple- Blacks who act like Asians

Popolo- Hiwaiian for "black person"

Red bone- Hi yellow, light skinned black

Rope head- Young black woman with braided weave hair

Salty- Angry over a minor issue or situation

Sneakers- Always come in pairs

Six- Good PC way to say nigger without getting jumped on. Can say "look at that 6 over there".

Tootsie roll- Black children

40- Forty oz of beer or some drink

925- LA Police code for suspicious person

Skag- Unattractive or promiscuous woman

Black gold- Oil

Word- "I understand you totally".   Juiced- to be excited.

Swag- Looking sharp, awesome   Wicked- it is "really good".

Flexing- Showing off

YOLO- You only live once

Meltdown- Total collapse

Pig out- Binge eating

Ratchet- Ugly, nasty appearance

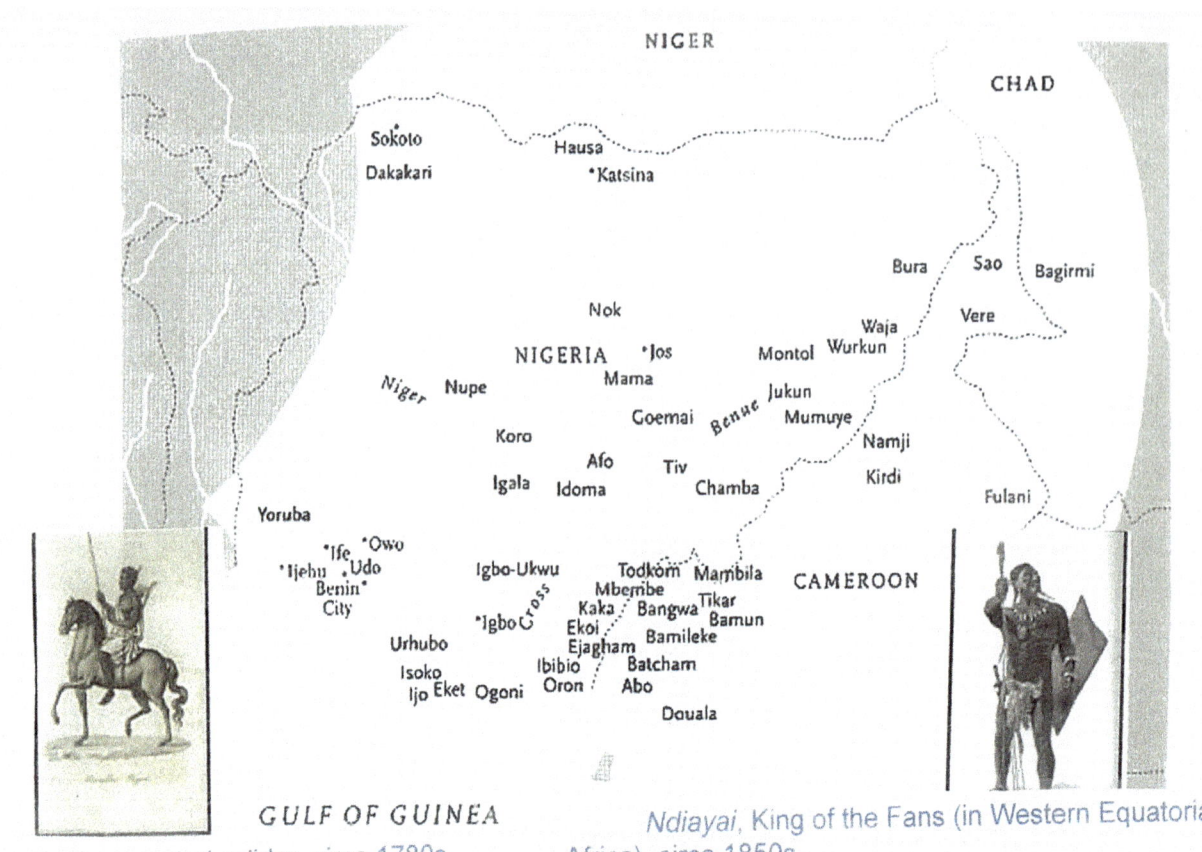

A horse-mounted solider, circa 1780s

Ndiayai, King of the Fans (in Western Equatorial Africa), circa 1850s

Tribal Maps of West Africa and Coastal West Africa

Slavery Isn't a Thing of the Past

Nicholas Kristof   NOV. 6, 2013

The movie "12 Years a Slave" is receiving rapturous reviews for depicting the antebellum South less as a gauzy land of elegant plantations than as the raw backdrop of monstrous brutality.

It's terrific that, in the 21st century, we can squarely face 19th-century slavery. But let's also acknowledge the modern versions of slavery in the world around us — and, yes, right here at home.

The United States is home to about 60,000 people who can fairly be called modern versions of slaves, according to a new Global Slavery Index released last month by the Walk Free Foundation, which fights human trafficking. These modern slaves aren't sold in chains in public auctions, so it's not exactly the same as 19th-century slavery. Those counted today include illegal immigrants forced to work without pay under threat of violence and teenage girls coerced to sell sex and hand all the money to their pimps.

99C

There are, of course, many more ambiguities today than in the 1850s about how to count slaves, but the slavery index finds almost 30 million people enduring modern slavery. More are in India than in any other country, and in some countries, such as Mauritania, children are still born into slavery.

Who are these modern American slaves?

One survivor I met last month in New Orleans, Clemmie Greenlee, had her life taken over by a pimp at age 12. She said she spent years having sex with up to 50 men a day. On average, she was beaten 10 times a month, for not meeting her daily quota or other offenses.

Why didn't she run away? Because, she says, of a mix of fear, Stockholm syndrome, emotional manipulation by pimps, hopelessness fueled by drug addiction and distrust of the authorities.

Eventually, Greenlee was able to escape that life, and she now runs a residential program called Eden House to help other women start over. An African-American, she says that what trafficked women endure is absolutely an echo of what her ancestors endured on plantations.

"If you're putting a whip on my back because I'm not picking enough cotton, or if you're beating me because I'm not earning my quota, it's the same thing," she said. "It's slavery."

Slavery isn't as formal or as widespread in the United States today as it was in the 1850s, of course, but it's still easy to find. Go to backpage.com, the leading website for prostitution advertising and search for your hometown. Some of the women selling sex there are adults voluntarily in the business, but many are women or girls under the control of pimps who take every penny they earn, brand them with tattoos and beat them if they don't earn enough.

Yet, in the United States, we typically arrest the victims rather than the pimps or the johns. Rectifying that would be a step toward modern emancipation.

The slavery index is the work of Andrew Forrest, an Australian billionaire who was awakened to the issue after his 15-year-old daughter, Grace, worked in an orphanage in Nepal. Grace later revisited the orphanage with her parents to check in on old friends — who were no longer there. They had, it turned out, been sold to brothels abroad.

After returning to Australia, Forrest ordered a review of his mining company's supply chains to make sure that there was no forced labor. He promptly found that some overseas laborers had had their passports confiscated and had gone unpaid for years. "With slavery experienced by my family and in my business, it was everywhere if you looked," he recalls, and he began a campaign against modern slavery.

Maybe we can find inspiration today not just from "12 Years a Slave," but also from the anti-slavery movement that began in Britain in the 1780s. It was one of the first great human rights campaigns in the world.

People then simply accepted slavery. The Bible encouraged slaves to be obedient, the Church of England owned a major slave plantation in Barbados and Thomas Jefferson advocated powerfully for human freedom except where slaves were involved.

That British abolitionist movement, pioneered by Quakers and led by Thomas Clarkson and William Wilberforce, with help from a former slave named Olaudah Equiano, caught fire and changed the world. Some 390,000 people, more people than were then eligible to vote in Britain, signed petitions against slavery. Hundreds of thousands of people boycotted sugar made with slave labor. It's a story movingly told by Adam Hochschild in his superb book "Bury the Chains."

The abolitionists succeeded in ending the trans-Atlantic slave trade, but their work is not finished. I fear that a century from now, someone may put together a movie about slavery in 2013, leading our descendants to shake their heads and ask of us: What were they thinking?

A version of this op-ed appears in print on November 7, 2013, on Page A33 of the New York edition with the headline: Slavery Isn't A Thing Of the Past.

Slavery Today

It isn't legal anywhere but happens almost everywhere—including Europe and the U.S. Slaves violence. They cannot walk away.

Slavery Is Everywhere

There are tens of millions of people trapped in various forms of slavery throughout the world today. Researchers estimate that 21 million are enslaved worldwide, generating $150 billion each year in illicit profits for traffickers.

- **Labor Slavery**. About 78 percent toil in forced labor slavery in industries where manual labor is needed—such as farming, ranching, logging, mining, fishing, and brick making—and in service industries working as dish washers, janitors, gardeners, and maids.
- **Sex Slavery**. About 22 percent are trapped in forced prostitution sex slavery.
- **Child Slavery**. About 26 percent of today's slaves are children.

Slavery today is a hidden crime, making it harder for the public to see and for those in slavery to call out for help.

Slavery statistics come from the U.N. International Labor Organization. See our Trafficking and Slavery Fact Sheet for details.

The Rise of Modern Slavery

Slavery has existed for thousands of years, but economic and social forces have enabled its alarming resurgence in the past few decades by increasing people's vulnerability.

- **Population**: A population explosion has tripled the number of people in the world, mostly in developing countries. In many places, the population has grown faster than the economy, leaving many people economically vulnerable. A fire, flood, drought, or medical emergency places them in the hands of ruthless moneylenders who enslave them.
- **Migration**: Millions are on the move from impoverished rural areas to cities, and from poorer countries to wealthier ones, in search of work. Traffickers are able to trick them by posing as legitimate labor recruiters. Migrants are especially vulnerable—they are often very far from home, don't speak the local language, have no funds to return home, and have no friends or family to rely on.
- **Corruption**: Global government corruption often allows slavery to go unpunished. Many law enforcement officials aren't even aware that bonded labor, where someone is enslaved to work off a loan, is illegal. In many places, those in slavery have no police protection from predatory traffickers.
- **Discrimination**: Social inequality creates widespread economic and social vulnerability based on factors such as gender, race, tribe, or caste.

Modern Slaves Are Cheap and Disposable

New slavery has two chief characteristics—it's cheap and it's disposable. Slaves today are cheaper than ever. In 1850, an average slave in the American South cost the equivalent of $40,000 in today's money. Today a slave costs about $90 on average worldwide. (*Source: Disposable People: New Slavery in the Global Economy. See all Free the Slaves books.*)

Modern slaves are not considered investments worth maintaining. In the 19th century it was difficult to capture slaves and transport them to the United States. But today, when someone in slavery gets sick or injured, they are simply dumped or killed.

The U.S. ranks 1st in prisoners

31 January 2015 MarkLeave a commentGo to comments

According to the International Centre for Prison Studies, there are 2,228,424 prisoners in the United States. That is enough to make the United States rank first in that category. The second highest number of prisoners is in China, at 1,701,344.

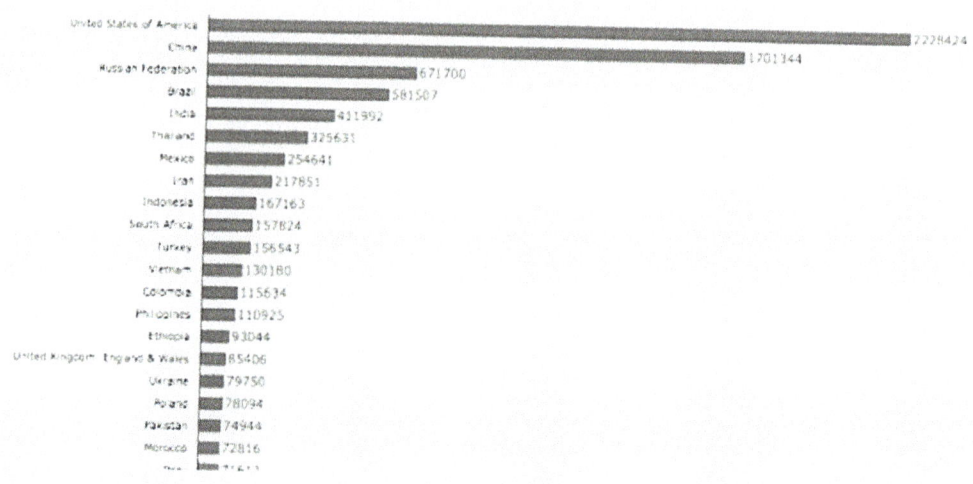

Chart from ICPS
http://www.prisonstudies.org/highest-to-lowest/prison-population-total?field_region_taxonomy_tid=All

99G

y. China ranks first, with 87% of Chinese saying that they are satisfied with how things are going in China.

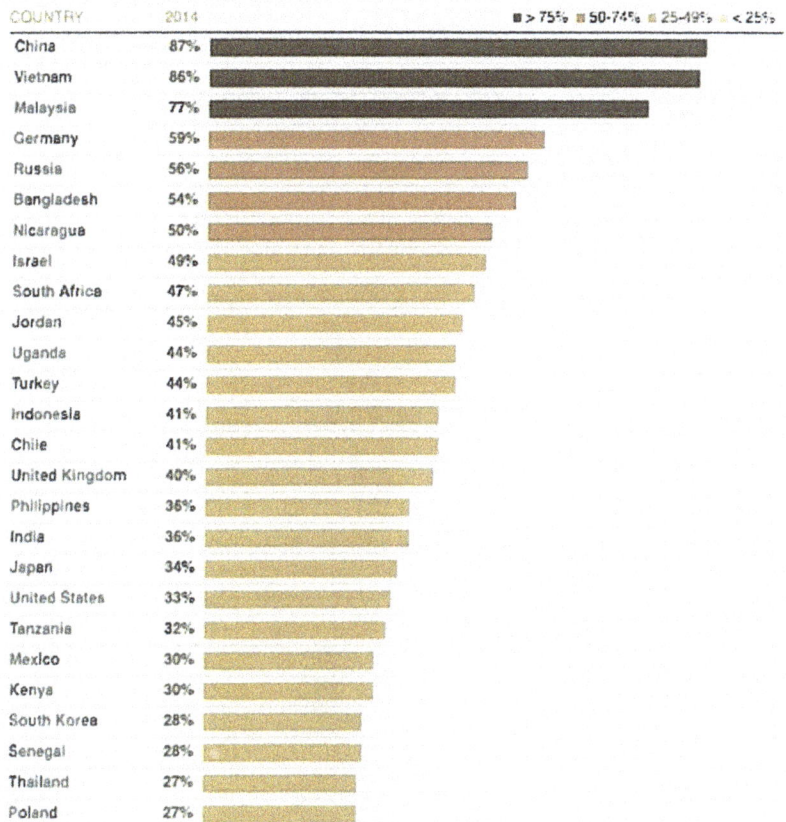

Chart from Pew
http://www.pewglobal.org/database/indicator/3/

Categories: Health and Welfare, Political and Social Life, Ranking of 11 to 20 Tags: China, Pew, satisfaction

In 23 Advanced Economies: U.S. Adults Rank 21st in Math Skills

In literacy, American adults achieved an average of 270 out of 500. That put Americans well ahead of Italy and Spain, whose adults scored 250 and 252, respectively, but far behind Japan and Finland, whose adults scored 296 and 288 respectively.

The NCES report said that among the American survey sample there were 112 people who were unable to complete even the survey's initial background questionnaire "because of a literacy-related barrier: either the inability to communicate in English or Spanish (the two languages in which the background questionnaire was administered) or a mental disability."

How 23 Advanced Economies Ranked in Numeracy:

1. Japan............................288

2. Finland.........................282

3. Flanders-Belgium........280

3. Netherlands..................280

5. Sweden........................279

6. Norway........................278

6. Denmark......................278

8. Slovak Republic...........276

8. Czech Republic...........276

10. Austria........................275

11. Estonia.......................273

12. Germany....................272

International average..269

13. Australia.....................268

14. Canada......................265

14, Cyprus......................265

16. Republic of Korea...263

17. United Kingdom......262

18. Poland......260

19. Ireland......256

20. France......254

21. United States..........253

22. Italy......247

23. Spain......246

How 23 Advanced Economies Ranked in Literacy:

1. Japan......296

2. Finland......288

3. Netherlands......284

4. Australia......280

5. Sweden......279

6. Norway......278

7. Estonia......276

8. Flanders-Belgium......275

9. Czech Republic......274

9. Slovak Republic......274

11. Canada......273

International average....273

12. Republic of Korea......273

13. United Kingdom......272

14. Denmark......271

15. Germany......270

15. United States..........270

17. Austria......269

17. Cyprus......269

19. Poland......267

19. Ireland......267

21. France......262

22. Spain......252

23. Italy......250

Illiteracy Statistics

U.S. Illiteracy Statistics	Data
Percent of U.S. adults who can't read (below a basic level)	14 %
Number of U.S. adults who can't read	32,000,000
Percent of prison inmates who can't read	70 %
Percent of high school graduates who can't read	19 %

Reading Level of U.S. Adults	Percent
Proficient	13 %
Intermediate	44 %
Basic	29 %
Below Basic	14 %

Demographics of Adults Who Read Below a Basic Level	Percent of Population
Hispanic	41 %
Black	24 %
White	9 %
Other	13 %

Global Illiteracy Statistics	Data
Number of people worldwide who can't read	775,000,000
Percent of the worlds illiterate who are female	66 %

Countries With the Highest Illiteracy Rates	Illiteracy Rate
South Sudan	73 %
Mali	72.3 %
Afghanistan	71.9 %
Niger	71.3 %
Burkina Faso	71.3 %

99K

NEW FBI STATS: BLACKS MORE LIKELY TO COMMIT HATE CRIMES THAN ANY OTHER RACE

DECEMBER 11, 2014 | BY BRIAN ANDERSON

We are told that because blacks are incarcerated at a disproportionate rate compared to their population that the criminal justice system is racist. We are told that because blacks are suspended from school at a disproportionate rate compared to their population that the education system is racist. Well, what are we to make of this: blacks commit hate crimes at a disproportionate rate to their population

The FBI just released the latest hate crime statistics and it doesn't look good for the black community, which is portrayed as America's biggest victim. In 2013 24.3% of all hate crime offenders were black. According to the last census, blacks make up 12.6% of the population. That means that blacks commit hate crimes at nearly double the rate of their population percentage.

Now let's compare that to whites: The FBI reports that 52.4% of hate crime offenders were white. Keep in mind that the FBI considers Hispanics as whites so the percentage of actual white hate crime offenders is likely much lower. In any case, non-Hispanic whites make up 63.7% of the US population. Throw in the Hispanics and it's 72.4%. Either way, whites commit hates crimes at a rate lower than their population percentage.

Here are the other races that the FBI keeps stats on with their hate crime and population percentages:

0.8% of offenders were Native American and Alaskan versus 0.9% of the population. It's close but still lower.

0.7% of offenders were Asian versus 4.8% of the population.

0.1% of offenders were Hawaiian or Pacific Islanders versus 0.2% of the population.

The only race that exceeds their population percentage in hate crime offenders are the blacks. If all things were equal, you'd think the numbers would match up.

BLACK VOICES   10/04/2013 03:24 pm ET | Updated Oct 04, 2013

1 In 3 Black Males Will Go To Prison In Their Lifetime, Report Warns

By Saki Knafo

GETTY

One in every three black males born today can expect to go to prison at some point in their life, compared with one in every six Latino males, and one in every 17 white males, if current incarceration trends continue.

These are among the many pieces of evidence cited by the Sentencing Project, a Washington, D.C.-based group that advocates for prison reform, in a report on the staggering racial disparities that permeate the American criminal justice system.

The report was submitted to the U.N. Human Rights Committee this week in advance of the U.N.'s review of American compliance with the International Covenant on Civil and Political Rights later this month. It argues that racial disparity pervades "every stage of the United States criminal justice system, from arrest to trial to sentencing."

TRENDING

Big Dog Makes Most Of His Tiny Bed

African American Health Disparities Compared to Non-Hispanic Whites

Racial and ethnic health disparities are undermining our communities and our health system. African Americans are more likely to suffer from certain health conditions, and they are more likely to get sicker, have serious complications, and even die from them. These are some of the more common health disparities that affect African Americans in the United States compared to non-Hispanic whites.

AFRICAN AMERICAN HEALTH DISPARITIES: ADULTS

depression
20% less likely to receive treatment for depression[1]

asthma
x2.1 as likely to die from asthma[2]

stroke
40% more likely to die from stroke[2]

breast cancer
40% more likely to die from breast cancer[2]

heart disease
30% more likely to die of heart disease[2]

cervical cancer
x2 as likely to die from cervical cancer[2]

obesity
40% more likely to be obese[3]

prostate cancer
x2 as likely to die from prostate cancer[2]

maternal mortality
x2.5 as likely to die during pregnancy[4]

HIV
x9 as likely to be diagnosed with HIV[6]
x8 as likely to die from HIV[2]

diabetes
60% more likely to be diabetic[3]
x2 as likely to undergo leg, foot, or toe amputation[5]

990

AFRICAN AMERICAN HEALTH DISPARITIES: CHILDREN

Compared to non-Hispanic white children, African American children are more likely to suffer from the following:

infant mortality
x2 as likely to die as an infant[7]

SIDS
x2 as likely to die of SIDS[2]

asthma
x2 as likely to have asthma[6]
x3 as likely to die from asthma[8]

obesity
73% more likely to be obese[9]

depression
30% more likely to attempt suicide as a high-schooler[10]

How do we reduce racial and ethnic health disparities? We must work together to improve our health care system to make it high-quality, comprehensive, affordable, and accessible for everyone.

April 2014 FamiliesUSA.org | **FAMILIES USA**

---

[1] Agency for Healthcare Research and Quality, 2012 National Healthcare Quality and Disparities Reports
[2] CDC, Deaths: Final Data for 2010
[3] CDC, Summary Health Statistics for U.S. Adults, National Health Interview Survey 2011
[4] CDC, Deaths: Final Data for 2007
[5] CDC, Age-Adjusted Hospital Discharge Rates for Nontraumatic Lower Extremity Amputations per 1,000 Diabetic Population, by Race, United States, 1988-2009
[6] CDC, National Center for HIV/AIDS, Viral Hepatitis, STD, and TB Prevention, Diagnoses of HIV Infection in the United States and Dependent Areas, 2011
[7] CDC, Infant Mortality Statistics from the 2009 Period Linked Birth/Infant Death Data Set
[8] CDC, National Surveillance of Asthma: United States, 2001-2010
[9] Federal Interagency Forum on Child and Family Statistics, America's Children: Key National Indicators of Well Being, 2013
[10] CDC, Youth Risk Behavior Surveillance – United States, 2011

Colonel Vaughan Witten, PhD
An autobiography of the innocence, happiness and final disappointment of a Virginia coal miner's son who sees his country on the slippery slope to immoral cultural destruction as he journeys from the coal fields to the military and highest le academia. This book describes the life and travels of a skinny, hard nosed, hard we West Virginia kid, a true believer in his family, the West Virginia-Appalachia cultu the goodness and righteousness of the United States of America. A rags to riches s a sort, from the primitive life of the coal fields to a Chief Master Sergeant in the Air and a PhD from a world class university.
He reveals a liberating journey and appreciation of his country while at the same time experiencing the slow decay of the American culture and values that he knew as a young man.

ISBN 0615432956
$49.

About the Author

(http://colonelvaughanwitten.com/about/)

Colonel Vaughan Witten was born on 18 February 1935 in Anawalt, West Virginia in a small coal mining village of about 2000 people, McDowell County. Born of wonderful parents, mother Arlene Walker Witten of Martinsville, VA., his father a coal miner and Baptist Minister Alphonso Witten of Anawalt, WV. Dr. Witten has five siblings Audrey (deceased), Sandra, Janita, James and Emma. Both mother and father passed away in 2000 and 1991 respectively. Dr. Witten was educated in a small one room schoolhouse with one teacher who taught six different grades in different corners of a small space. After grade school, he graduated from Washington High School in London, WV at the age of 15. He joined the Air Force at age 17 and served 27 years, including three tours in Vietnam and duty in Thailand, Japan, Greenland, Iceland, Greece, Portugal, The Azores and the Philippines. He earned the Bronze Star and achieved the highest enlisted rank of Command Chief Master Sergeant.

On the academic side of his life, Dr. Witten acquired two BA Degrees from Shaw University and North Carolina State University, and a PhD in Psychology from North Carolina State in 1989. After retiring from the Air Force, he taught psychology and sociology as a professor at Park College, Webster University and Shaw University for 34 years. Now fully retired, he spends his time learning foreign languages, welding, wood building, forklift driving, art and much more. To remain active, he also enjoys mountain bike riding and frequents numerous parks and the hills of North Carolina and West Virginia. Dr. Witten, having absorbed the blows of the death of both parents and the recent death of his beloved wife Mildred after 50 years of marriage, provides through his episodic journey the thrill, wonder, joy, pain and appreciation of his life in Appalachia –a virtual paradise on earth provided by God, family and America– and finally the despair of a virtual Purgatory in a declining, immoral, decadent culture that he perceives devolving before his eyes in America.

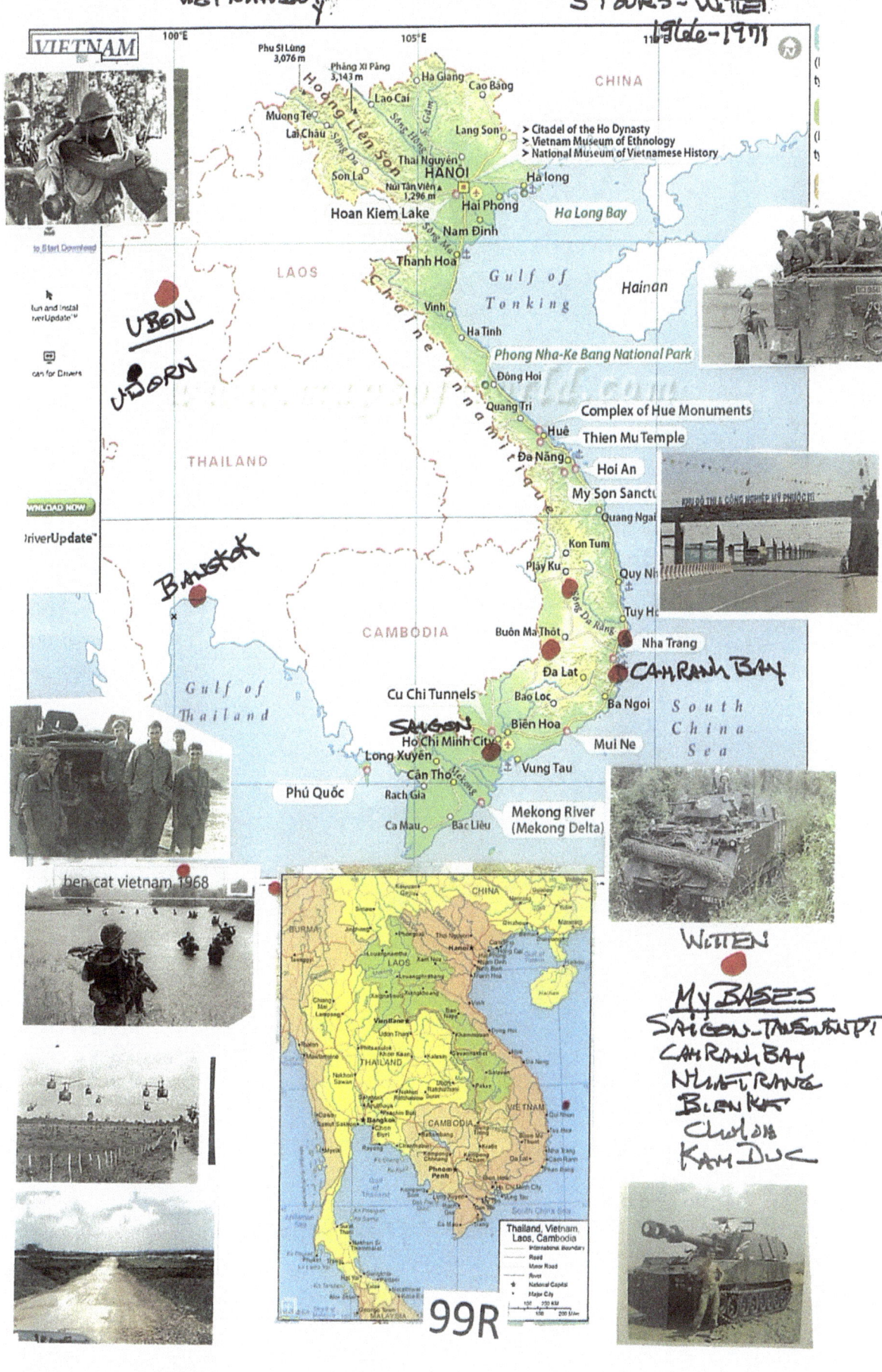

● BASES + TDY - WITT

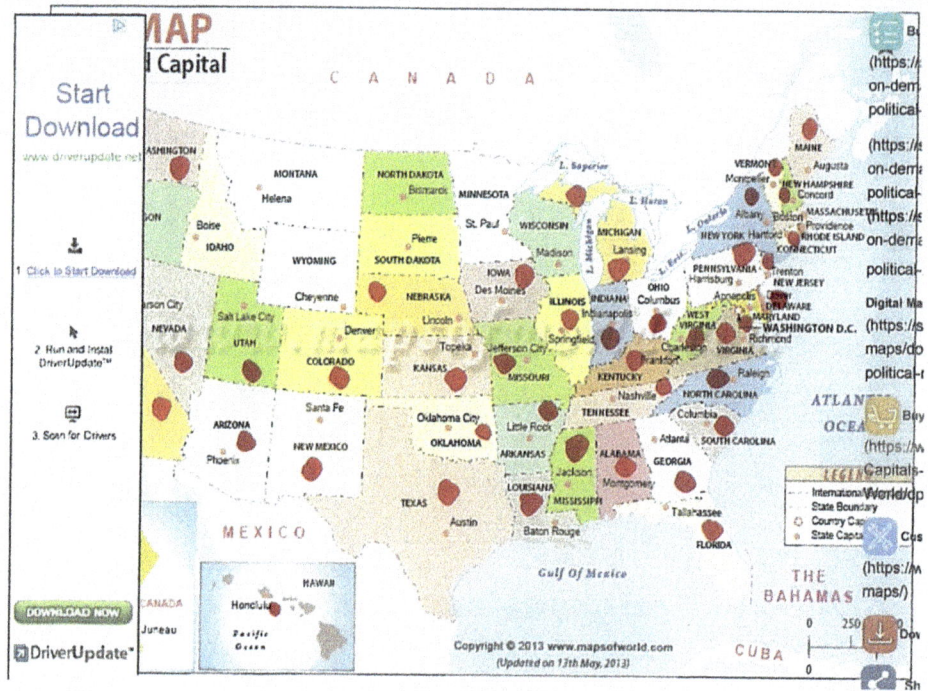

● STATES VISITED - WITTEN

99S

REFERENCES

African American Population Report (2010), <u>Elementary, High School and College Education of Blacks</u>. Black Demographics.com.

Allen, David, MD. (2014) <u>Fear of success masquerading as fear of failure. A Matter of persuasion,</u> Psychology Today.

Anyiam, T. (2007) <u>Who should jump the broom</u>. Anyiams Creations International.

Bandler, Aaron, (2016) <u>Black on Black Crime,</u> Daily Wire.

Bass, Karen, (2013) <u>State of emergency for Black youth and education,</u> LA Watts Times.

Boa, F. (2017) Does culture affect our personality? Explorable.com.

Bond J. et al,(2000) "Lift every voice and sing- 100 years old". Random House.

Bruner, J. (1974) Readings in Cross Cultural Psychology ed. JLM Dawkins et al pp 381-91, Hong Kong University Press.

Clayborn, Carson, et al, (2012), The struggle for freedom: A history of African Americans. Prentice Hall.

Cole, Juan, (2017) How America has failed African American youth by the numbers. Mic Daily.com.

Cook, Linsay, (2015) U.S. Education: Still

Separate and unequal. U.S. News.

Edwards, William. (2017) <u>Journal of Black Higher Education</u>.

Feierman, Lisa, (2014) <u>Troubling Statistics for African American males in the classroom.</u> Google www.

Friedman, Russell, (2012) <u>Fear of failure fear of success.</u> Psychology Today 2012.

Funder, J. (1997) <u>The personality puzzle,</u> New York. Norton.

Ghost, T.J. (2013) <u>The cold hard truth about Black culture.</u> Dairy www-Google.

Glaude, E. (2014) <u>African American Studies,</u> Princeton University Press.

Gomez, M.A. (1998) <u>Exchanging our country marks: The transformation of Africans identities in the colonial and Antebellum South</u>. University of North Carolina Press.

Hicks, D.S. (2014) <u>An unusual feast: Gumbo and the complex brew of Black Religion</u>. Columbia University Press.

Hicks, Mack. (2014) <u>Digital Pandemic</u>- Psychology Today.

Journal of Black Psychology (2016) <u>Comparison of Helplessness and Hopelessness-Cognitive vulnerability among Black and White college students</u>. Google www.

Lee, T. (1999) *Why study personality in culture?* pp 3-22.

Maccoby, E. E. (2000) *Parenting and its effect on children: On reading and mis-reading behavior genetics.* Annual Review Psychology.

McCrae, R.R (2000) *Trait psychology and the revival of personality and culture studies.* American Behavioral Science.

MacDonald, (2015) *War on Cops.*

Marano, Hara. (2016) *The fear of success* www Psychology Today.com.

Moore, A. (2013) *5 Reasons young Black men resort to violence.* Atlanta Black Star.

Moskowitz, C. (2010) Baby names reveal more about parents than ever before. www Live Science.com.

Payne, J. (2007) "Dying for basic care" www Washington Post.

Rohner, R.R. (1986) The warmth dimension: Foundations of parental acceptance-Rejection theory. Newbury Park, CA. Sage.

Saki, Knafo, (2013) Black voices. Google.

Schweder, R.A. (1991) Rethinking culture and personality theory. Cambridge MA. Harvard University Press.

Sowell, Thomas. (2012) Race, IQ, Black crime and facts liberals ignore. Opin Jrnl.

Tesfailiariam, Rachel. (2012) <u>Understanding the root causes of Black violence</u>. Washington Post.

Thompson, Tamika. (2016) <u>Fact Sheet: Outcomes for young Black men</u>. Tavis Smiley Reports on PBS.

Thorn, Victor. (2014) <u>Journal of Crime and Delinquency,</u> www Internet.

Triandis and Suh. (2002) <u>Cultural Influences on Personality.</u> Annual Review Psychology 2002.

U.S. Department of Education. (2009) <u>Black-White student achievement gap persists</u>. Associated Press.

Wattenburg, L. (2013) The Baby Name

Wizard. Revised 3rd ed. A magical way for finding the perfect name for your baby.com.

Williams, Walter. (2017) Grossly poor educated students.

Witkin, H.A. (1979) Socialization, culture and ecology in the development of group and sex differences in cognitive styles. Human Development, 22, 358-372.

Witkin, H.A. (1974) Social Conformity and Psychological differentiation. International Journal of Psychology 9, 11-25.

Witten, Colonel V. (1989) Field Dependence-Field Independence: The relationship of cognitive style and academic achievement. N.C. State University Press, Raleigh.

Witten, Colonel V. (2017) Black Escape from Freedom. Self Published, Fayetteville N.C.

Witten, Colonel V. (2013) The Journey: Appalachia to Paradise to Purgatory. An autobiography. A Place to Copy, Raleigh, N.C.

Wooldridge, Frosty. (2008) Multiculturalism-Destroying American culture. www Rense.com.

www.ingramcontent.com/pod-product-compliance
Lightning Source LLC
Chambersburg PA
CBHW061358010526
44107CB00012B/971